WILL YOU HEAR MY CONFESSION?

Originally published in Spanish under the title *Quiero Confessarme* by Ediciones Paulinas, Florida, 1981.

WILL YOU HEAR MY CONFESSION?

How to Make a Good Examination of Conscience and a Good Confession

Friar Hector Munoz, O.P.

Translated by Robert R. Barr

ALBA · HOUSE   NEW · YORK

SOCIETY OF ST. PAUL, 2187 VICTORY BLVD., STATEN ISLAND, NEW YORK 10314

Library of Congress Cataloging in Publication Data

Muñoz, Héctor, O.P.
  Will you hear my confession.

  "Originally published in Spanish under the title
Quiero confessarme by Ediciones Paulinas, Florida, 1981."
    1. Conscience, Examination of. 2. Confession.
3.Catholic Church—Prayer-books and devotions—
English. 1. Title.
BX2377.M8613   1982   265'.61   82-20597
ISBN 0-8189-0439-9

Nihil Obstat:
Thomas M. O'Hagan, S.L.L.
Censor Librorum

Imprimatur:
†Joseph T. O'Keefe, D.D.
Vicar General
Archdiocese of New York
November 20, 1982

Designed, printed and bound in the United States of
America by the Fathers and Brothers of the
Society of St. Paul, 2187 Victory Boulevard,
Staten Island, New York 10314, as part of their
communications apostolate.

1 2 3 4 5 6 7 8 9 (Current Printing: first digit)

Contents

Contents

Introduction

This book seeks to reach believers' minds, that they may know what God has in store for those who love him and those he loves. It seeks to touch their hearts, to move them in the right direction. It seeks to show us that the Christian life is a life of conversion. It seeks to steer us by the right course, as we battle the deep, invisible currents that brutally (or subtly) beat us away from our destination or try to slow our passage.

But it is not a matter of merely striving not to be evil. It is a matter of becoming saints. This is our vocation—the vocation of all those whom the Father seeks to convert, gathering them around his Incarnate Son. It is the vocation of all of us who are Church.

And so, being converted will be nothing but knowing, imitating, and following Jesus. We shall have to see what our Lord said and did, what his virtues were, how he dialogued with human beings, and what value he placed on the world. We shall want to know why he spoke as he did, and why he acted as the Gospel shows us he did. St. Augustine said, "The human being we saw with our eyes"—Jesus—"was not the model we were to imitate. The model we were to imitate was God. But we could not see him with our eyes. And this is why God became a human being—to place before our eyes a model we could see and could imitate."

Jesus Christ is the model God used to reveal himself so that we could follow him. Christ is the "meeting place" where God and human beings see each other. Christian morality, then, in view of what we have said, will be an "evangelical morality"—a Gospel morality, firmly based on the words and works of our Lord. The Apostles made these words and works explicit by their lives and by their teaching, and left us a clear and complete doctrinal structure.

If we made a move of someone's life, and then looked at the film itself, the celluloid—every little square we would see would be a scene from his or her life. It would be a part of that person's story. Perhaps the subject of the film might be ourselves, and each scene would represent part of our own story. There would be enchanting pictures there—moments of grace. But some of the pictures would be a little fuzzy, a bit out of focus. And then there would be scenes we would wish had never been filmed. We would relive our sorrows and our joys. We would recall little slips, and abysmal falls, and climbs to the heights. Our memory would bring back times of fidelity, and hours of apostasy.

If we watched this film in truth and wisdom, we would see a variety of wounds we have inflicted on our brothers and sisters, as well as on ourselves. The blood from these wounds would keep our eyes riveted to these offenses to God. Of course, our memory would also recall hurts done us by others.

Well . . . everyone has this film at home!

The examination of conscience proposed in this book is not meant to be made on a purely psychological level. It is meant to give the reader a Christian vision of grace and sin—a hope-filled vision, in which every prodigal son and daughter may know that the Father is waiting at the bend of the road, anxious, waiting to array his child in the finest garments and take him or her back home again.

This book is intended to help us make a good confession. Without scruples, but with delicacy of conscience. Without servile fear, but with a holy "fear of God." With respect, but without shriveling up inside. With familiarity, but in the knowledge that "Jesus Christ is Lord." With confidence in God's mercy but without any desire to abuse it. With the freshness and simplicity of children, but with a desire to grow to an adult faith. With a right understanding of God, in order to love him and live in his grace. With a deep sense of sin, in order to hate it and flee it. With a certitude that God does not reject sinners, for it is he who has forged in us this humble and contrite heart, this desire to return to him. With the certainty that Christ's blood has not been spilled in vain, and that his mercy is greater than our miseries.

By following the questions and answers in this book step by step, as we make our "examination of conscience," we shall not only be preparing ourselves for sacramental confession, we shall be making an evangelical review of our life as well. We shall discover that the best way to prepare for confession is to try to discern, by looking at Christ, whether *my* words and deeds in the story of *my* life are like *his* words and deeds in the story of *his* life. After all, he spoke them and performed them in order that we might be able to have "traces of God," as the Fathers of the Church used to call them, in the history of human beings. God's will is to transform the history of men and women into sacred history, into *his* history—into "salvific history."

The whole examination should be made responsibly and voluntarily, in the liberty of the daughters and sons of God, for it is the Spirit who moves us to make it. We must make it in living truth—in truth about life that will make us free. For we are liberated *by* this truth, and we are liberated *for* this truth—liberated for a love that bears witness that this truth, and this life, are true indeed.

As we have said, in writing this book we have sought to root these examinations clearly in the life of Christ and in his teaching. In this way our Christian morality will be an evangelical morality—a morality of the Gospel, a morality based on the word and example of Christ our Model. The questions in the "examination in the light of evangelical and apostolic teaching" will be based on the witness of the life of Jesus and his first disciples, and on what they have left us by way of an example and model for our imitation. In this fashion, our efforts to be converted will always be made in the sight of God, as we judge and forgive ourselves as he judges and forgives us.

Now let us think about reconciliation. And let us examine our consciences.

WILL YOU HEAR MY CONFESSION?

Chapter 1

The Sacrament of Reconciliation in the Present Teaching of the Church

This book is intended as a help to make a good examination of conscience. Now, a good examination of conscience is not just any sort of examination you please. For example, it is not a rooting around in our spiritual innards in order to be able to describe just how weak and fallible we are. It is a matter of reading our heart as Christ reads it. It is a matter of discovering our fragility before the impeccability of an absolutely sinless Lord. It is a matter of placing our miseries face to face with the mercy of God—not so as to fall into despair because we are not as God, but in order to give an account of our faith and our hope: to believe and to know that we are strong in our weakness, because God has erected his fortress in this creaturely clay of ours.

Therefore we shall begin by reproducing the whole first two parts of the Introduction to the new Rite of Penance. By reading this material carefully and attentively, we shall gain an insight into this sacramental reality of Christ and the Church—the place where God's pardon and human beings' need for pardon come together. If we *know what we are about*, the examination of conscience can be very enlightening, and bear much fruit.

I—The Mystery of Reconciliation in the History of Salvation
1. The Father has shown forth his mercy by reconciling the world to himself in Christ and by making peace for all things on earth and in heaven by the blood of Christ on the cross.[1] The Son of God made man lived among men in order to free them from the slavery of sin[2] and to call

them out of darkness into his wonderful light.[3] He therefore began his work on earth by preaching repentance and saying: "Turn away from sin and believe the good news" (Mk 1:15). This invitation to repentance, which had often been sounded by the prophets, prepared the hearts of men for the coming of the Kingdom of God through the voice of John the Baptist who came "preaching a baptism of repentance for the forgiveness of sins" (Mk 1:4).

Jesus, however, not only exhorted men to repentance so that they should abandon their sins and turn wholeheartedly to the Lord,[4] but he also welcomed sinners and reconciled them with the Father.[5] Moreover, by healing the sick he signified his power to forgive sin.[6] Finally, he himself died for our sins and rose again for our justification.[7] Therefore, on the night he was betrayed and began his saving passion,[8] he instituted the sacrifice of the new covenant in his blood for the forgiveness of sins.[9] After his resurrection he sent the Holy Spirit upon the apostles, empowering them to forgive or retain sins[10] and sending them forth to all peoples to preach repentance and the forgiveness of sins in his name.[11]

The Lord said to Peter, "I will give you the keys of the kingdom of heaven, and whatever you bind on earth will be bound in heaven, and whatever you loose on earth will be loosed also in heaven" (Mt 16:19). In obedience to this command, on the day of Pentecost, Peter preached the forgiveness of sins by baptism: "Repent and let every one of you be baptized in the name of Jesus Christ for the forgiveness of your sins" (Ac 2:38).[12] Since then the Church has never failed to call men from sin to conversion and by the celebration of penance to show the victory of Christ over sin.

2. This victory is first brought to light in baptism where our fallen nature is crucified with Christ so that the body of sin may be destroyed and we may no longer be slaves to sin, but rise with Christ and live for God.[13] For this reason the Church proclaims its faith in "the one baptism for the forgiveness of sins."

In the sacrifice of the Mass the passion of Christ is made present; his body given for us and his blood shed for the forgiveness of sins are offered to God again by the Church for the salvation of the world. In the Eucharist Christ is present and is offered as "the sacrifice which has made our peace"[14] with God and in order that "we may be brought together in unity"[15] by his Holy Spirit.

Furthermore our Savior Jesus Christ, when he gave to his apostles and their successors power to forgive sins, instituted in his Church the sacrament of penance. Thus the faithful who fall into sin after baptism may be reconciled with God and renewed in grace.[16] The Church "possesses both water and tears: the water of baptism, the tears of penance."[17]

II—The Reconciliation of Penitents in the Church's Life

THE CHURCH IS HOLY BUT ALWAYS IN NEED OF PURIFICATION

3. Christ "loved the Church and gave himself up for her to make her holy" (Ep 5:25-26), and he united the Church to himself as his bride.[18] He filled her with his divine gifts,[19] because she is his body and fullness, and through her he spreads truth and grace to all.

The members of the Church, however, are exposed to temptation and unfortunately often fall into sin. As a result, "while Christ, 'holy, innocent, and unstained' (Heb 7:26), did not know sin (2 Cor 5:21) but came only to atone for the sins of the people (see Heb 2:17), the Church, which includes within itself sinners and is at the same time holy and always in need of purification, constantly pursues repentance and renewal."[20]

PENANCE IN THE CHURCH'S LIFE AND LITURGY

4. The people of God accomplishes and perfects this continual repentance in many different ways. It shares in the suffering of Christ[21] by enduring its own difficulties, carries out works of mercy and charity,[22] and adopts ever more fully the outlook of the Gospel message. Thus the people of God becomes in the world a sign of conversion to God. All this the Church expresses in its life and celebrates in the liturgy when the faithful confess that they are sinners and ask pardon of God and of their brothers and sisters. This happens in penitential services, in the proclamation of the word of God, in prayer, and in the penitential aspects of the eucharistic celebration.[23]

In the sacrament of penance the faithful "obtain from the mercy of God pardon for their sins against him; at the same time they are reconciled with the Church which they wounded by their sins and which works for their conversion by charity, example, and prayer."[24]

RECONCILIATION WITH GOD AND WITH THE CHURCH

5. Since every sin is an offense against God which disrupts our friendship with him, "the ultimate purpose of penance is that we should love God deeply and commit ourselves completely to him."[25] Therefore, the sinner who by the grace of a merciful God embraces the way of penance comes back to the Father who "first loved us" (1 Jn 4:19), to Christ who gave himself up for us,[26] and to the Holy Spirit who has been poured out on us abundantly.[27]

"By the hidden and loving mystery of God's design men are joined together in the bonds of supernatural solidarity, so much so that the sin of one harms the others just as the holiness of one benefits the others."[28] Penance always entails reconciliation with our brothers and sisters who are always harmed by our sins.

In fact, men frequently join together to commit injustice. It is thus only fitting that they should help each other in doing penance so that they who are freed from sin by the grace of Christ may work with all men of good will for justice and peace in the world.

THE SACRAMENT OF PENANCE AND ITS PARTS

6. The follower of Christ who has sinned but who has been moved by the Holy Spirit to come to the sacrament of penance should above all be converted to God with his whole heart. This inner conversion of heart embraces sorrow for sin and the intent to lead a new life. It is expressed through confession made to the Church, due satisfaction, and amendment of life. God grants pardon for sin through the Church, which works by the ministry of priests.[29]

a) Contrition

The most important act of the penitent is contrition, which is "heartfelt sorrow and aversion for the sin committed along with the intention of sinning no more."[30] "We can only approach the Kingdom of Christ by *metanoia*. This is a profound change of the whole person by which one begins to consider, judge, and arrange his life according to the holiness and love of God, made manifest in his Son in the last days and given to us in abundance" (see Heb 1:2; Col 1:19 and *passim*).[31] The genuineness of penance depends on this heartfelt contrition. For conversion should affect a person from within so that it may progressively enlighten him and render him continually more like Christ.

b) Confession

The sacrament of penance includes the confession of sins, which comes from true knowledge of self before God and from contrition for those sins. However, this inner examination of heart and the exterior accusation should be made in the light of God's mercy. Confession requires in the penitent the will to open his heart to the minister of God, and in the minister a spiritual judgment by which, acting in the person of Christ, he pronounces his decision of forgiveness or retention of sins in accord with the power of the keys.[32]

c) Act of Penance (Satisfaction)

True conversion is completed by acts of penance or satisfaction for the sins committed, by amendment of conduct, and also by the reparation of injury.[33] The kind and extent of the satisfaction should be suited to the personal condition of each penitent so that each one may restore the order which he disturbed and through the corresponding remedy be cured of the sickness from which he suffered. Therefore, it is necessary that the act of penance really be a remedy for sin and a help to renewal of life. Thus the penitent, "forgetting the things which are behind him" (Ph 3:13), again becomes part of the mystery of salvation and turns himself toward the future.

d) Absolution

Through the sign of absolution God grants pardon to the sinner who in sacramental confession manifests his change of heart to the Church's minister, and thus the sacrament of penance is completed. In God's design the humanity and loving kindness of our Savior have visibly appeared to us,[34] and God uses visible signs to give salvation and to renew the broken covenant.

In the sacrament of penance the Father receives the repentant son who comes back to him, Christ places the lost sheep on his shoulders and brings it back to the sheepfold, and the Holy Spirit sanctifies this temple of God again or lives more fully within it. This is finally expressed in a renewed and more fervent sharing of the Lord's table, and there is great joy at the banquet of God's Church over the son who has returned from afar.[35]

THE NECESSITY AND BENEFIT OF THE SACRAMENT

7. Just as the wound of sin is varied and multiple in the life of individuals and of the community, so too the healing which penance provides is varied. Those who by grave sin have withdrawn from the communion of love with God are called back in the sacrament of penance to the life they have lost. And those who through daily weakness fall into venial sins draw strength from a repeated celebration of penance to gain the full freedom of the children of God.

a) To obtain the saving remedy of the sacrament of penance, according to the plan of our merciful God, the faithful must confess to a priest each and every grave sin which they remember upon examination of conscience.[36]

b) Moreover, frequent and careful celebration of this sacrament is also very useful as a remedy for venial sins. This is not a mere ritual repetition or psychological exercise, but a serious striving to perfect the grace of baptism so that, as we bear in our body the death of Jesus Christ, his life may be seen in us ever more clearly.[37] In confession of this kind, penitents who accuse themselves of venial faults should try to conform more closely to Christ and to follow the voice of the Spirit more attentively.

In order that this sacrament of healing may truly achieve its purpose among Christ's faithful, it must take root in their whole lives and move them to more fervent service of God and neighbor.

The celebration of this sacrament is thus always an act in which the Church proclaims its faith, gives thanks to God for the freedom with which Christ has made us free,[38] and offers its life as a spiritual sacrifice in praise of God's glory, as it hastens to meet the Lord Jesus.

Footnotes

1. See 2 Cor 5:18ff; Col 1:20.
2. See Jn 8:34-36.
3. See 1 P 2:9.
4. See Lk 15.
5. Lk 5:20, 27-32; 7:48.

6. See Mt 9:2-8.
7. See Rm 4:25.
8. See Roman Missal, Eucharistic Prayer III.
9. See Mt 26:28.
10. See Jn 20:19-23.
11. See Lk 24:47.
12. See Ac 3:19, 26; 17:30.
13. See Rm 6:4-10.
14. Roman Missal, Eucharistic Prayer III.
15. Roman Missal, Eucharistic Prayer II.
16. See Council of Trent, Session XIV, De sacramento Paenitentiae, Chapter I: Denz.-Schön. 1668 and 1670; can. 1: Denz.-Schön. 1701.
17. St. Ambrose, Letter 41:12: *PL* 16, 1116.
18. See Rv 19:7.
19. See Ep 1:22-23; Second Vatican Council, constitution *Lumen gentium*, no. 7: *AAS* 57 (1965) 9-11.
20. Second Vatican Council, constitution *Lumen gentium*, no. 8: *ibid.*, 12.
21. See 1 P 4:13.
22. See 1 P 4:8.
23. See Council of Trent, Session XIV, De Sacramento Paenitentiae: Denz.-Schön. 1638, 1740, 1743; Congregation of Rites, instruction *Eucharisticum mysterium*, May 25, 1967, no. 35: *AAS* 59 (1967) 560-561; Roman Missal, *General Instruction*, nos. 29, 30, 56 a.b.g.
24. Second Vatican Council, constitution *Lumen gentium*, no. 11: *AAS* 57 (1965) 15-16.
25. Paul VI, Apostolic Constitution *Paenitemini*, February 17, 1966: *AAS* 58 (1966) 179; See Second Vatican Council, constitution *Lumen gentium*, no. 11: *AAS* 57 (1965) 15-16.
26. See Gal 2:20; Ep 5:25.
27. See Tit 3:6.
28. Paul VI, Apostolic Constitution *Indulgentiarum doctrina*, January 1, 1967, no. 4: *AAS* 59 (1967) 9; see Pius XII, encyclical *Mystici Corporis*, June 29, 1943: *AAS* 35 (1943) 213.
29. See Council of Trent, Session XIV, De sacramento Paenitentiae, Chapter I: Denz.-Schön. 1673-1675.
30. *Ibid.*, Chapter 4: Denz.-Schön. 1676.
31. Paul VI, Apostolic Constitution Paenitemini, February 17, 1966: *AAS* 58 (1966) 179.
32. See Council of Trent, Session XIV, De sacramento Paenitentiae, Chapter 5: Denz.-Schön. 1679.
33. See Council of Trent, Session XIV, De sacramento Paenitentiae, Chapter 8: Denz.-Schön. 1690-1692; Paul VI, Apostolic Constitution *Indulgentiarum doctrina*, January 1, 1967, nos. 2-3: *AAS* 59 (1967) 6-8.
34. See Tit 3:4-5.
35. See Lk 15:7, 10, 32.
36. See Council of Trent, Session XIV, De sacramento Paenitentiae, can. 7-8: Denz.-Schön. 1707-1708.
37. See 2 Cor 4:10.
38. See Gal 4:31.

Chapter 2

Forms for Examining Our Conscience

At the end of the Ritual of Penance, after having explained the Sacrament, prescribed its Rite, and given a number of suggestions for Reconciliation Services and prayers and readings for our meditation, the Church offers us a "Form of Examination of Conscience" to help us prepare to receive the Sacrament. It consists of sets of questions which we may ask ourselves in the light of God's grace.

We shall now reproduce these sets of questions—with a little meditation after each set, so that we may be better helped to answer them before God. First, the Church proposes we ask ourselves three sets of questions concerning the Sacrament of Penance itself, and our attitude toward it. Then come the questions for the examination of conscience.

First, then, let us ask ourselves what our attitude is, and has been, toward the Sacrament of Penance.

A. General Examination on the Sacrament of Penance

1. What is my attitude to the sacrament of penance? Do I sincerely want to be set free from sin, to turn again to God, to begin a new life, and to enter into a deeper friendship with God? Or do I look on it as a burden, to be undertaken as seldom as possible?

Let us think about these questions, and how we shall answer them.

One thing that is asked of us, then, is *sincerity*. Our desire must be sincere. This means that we could be insincere—that frankness and honesty could be missing from our desire. And this is to be avoided. There is nothing worse than pharisaism—the attitude that keeps our heart divided in two within us, almost (to use an analogy) as if we were spiritual schizophrenics. True, the old self will always war against the new self. But this does not mean that we must not strive, with determination, to be on our guard against all duplicity, so that we may present ourselves to God as we are—the only way to be able to see him as he is.

In what does this sincere desire consist? There are several essential elements for us to consider: purification, conversion, renewal, and friendship.

Purification is the removal of the dross, or slag, from our mind and heart, so that only the pure metal remains. But this purification has a price—fire. In the smelting process, metallic ore is subjected to fire. Little by little the impurities are burned away, leaving only the precious material. The soul, too, has need of fire. And fire burns. More often than not, the therapy is painful and slow. Our purification treatment can be painful, and last a long time. There is the risk of falling into despair, like a sick person who thinks he or she will never get well.

Conversion means I must leave a situation which my conscience declares is evil, and move to another, which my conscience, corrected in the light of the Gospel, tells me is good. Conversion means changing course. At times this change will have to be total and radical. At other times it will be enough just to tap the rudder a bit in order to correct a slight deviation from our course. But of course in either case, the deflection, little or great, turns me away from my port of destination. And we know from experience—our own and that of others—that a small deviation in the beginning, if left uncorrected, gradually moves me further and further off course.

Here I should like to repeat something important I have said—this time about conversion. Conversion is not a matter of just some change or other. Conversion is a change that makes me see life, and the story of my life, from a Gospel viewpoint. It is a change that makes me see life, and my life, with the eyes of Christ.

Renewal means making something new again. Now if we make something new again, it must have gotten old. To make a good examination of conscience in order to go to confession, we have to desire the new life of the "new self"—the absolute newness that Jesus offers us so that the "old Adam" within us may finish dying. This is a difficult thing. But it is not impossible. Only the new self is capable of infecting all things with its newness, thereby rescuing the history of human beings from its feebleness, its routiness, and its poverty.

Friendship: Not every sin causes us to lose God's friendship. This misfortune occurs only in the case of serious sins. Just as some little act of inconsiderateness does not cause us to lose a friend, so neither does a slight sin break the ties that bind us to our most excellent Friend. But it is by no means enough merely not to sin gravely against our Lord. We may not sit back and take our ease just because we are "not evil persons." God has given us a vocation: to be holy as he is holy. Accordingly, we should be spurred on by the desire of a *deeper* friendship with him. For the law for a Christian is always to go further and higher—to do more, and to do better. Our goal should be a friendship which will be a fitting return of God's love. And "only they arrive who do not faint on the way."

The negative side of the question we are asking is whether we consider confession a task, a heavy load someone has placed on our shoulders—something "the priests have invented" to keep us human beings in a state of dependency, as if we were minors. I don't go to confession because "I don't get anything out of it," or because "I don't like to go," or because "I don't see why I have to confess my sins to a human being," or because "priests are sinners too, and I don't see what right they have to know my sins" . . . and so on and on.

If this is the case, of course then I shall go to confession "when I feel like it," or "when I feel I need it" or when I see myself assaulted by life's heavy blows and "I don't feel good" about myself, or when social or family pressures force me to go. "How can you deprive your little girl of the joy of seeing you receive when she makes her First Communion?" Or perhaps one of the children is getting married, or you have a funeral Mass to attend. At times like these a still, small voice deep inside my conscience will tell me, "You mustn't go to Communion unless you go to confession first"—and so I pop into church for a couple of minutes when confessions are going on, practically always poorly prepared, with my act of reconciliation bound up with something or someone who in one way or another has nothing to do with the deeper motives that should move a man or woman to kneel before God and tell him that he or she is a poor sinner. Not that we deny that God in his loving providence can make use of such an occasion to give a person the grace to come back to him. But we have no right to rely on the extraordinary. We have a duty to exercise habitual discernment of heart.

2. Did I forget to mention, or deliberately conceal, any grave sins in past confessions?

When the Church asks us to make an "integral confession of our grave sins," it does not do so lightly or thoughtlessly, or in order to burden our consciences with an impossible examination. Nor are we being asked to rummage around in the very bottom of our being as if we were picking through the contents of a garbage can. Nothing could be further from the peace which Christ and his Church desire for the person who approaches the Sacrament of Reconciliation. This is the great moment of pardon, peace, and freedom.

But we do have to be careful not to deceive ourselves. More than one person has been known to make his or her confession sound like a litany of virtues. Even in good actions there can be a measure of vainglory. May the joy we feel from confessing our sins be from God's wiping away our miseries, and not from how good I am, how humble I am, or how penitent I am.

When we go to confession, first we must make an examination of conscience that *is* truly "conscious" and possesses self-awareness— which is what the word "conscience" means—and is made in a serious, adult manner, without any attempt to do more than a normal human being can do with a good memory, but without doing less, either. We should ask the Spirit to aid our understanding and our memory—not so much so as to be able to say we recall everything we have done every instant over the past month, but so as to be able to take full account of our Lord's footsteps as he walks beside me along the road of this life, and then to take account of the steps we have taken on our own initiative without consider-ing the Companion of our journey because we wanted to hide from the God who was looking for us.

The point is not to perform an exercise in memory (although we must, of course, perform one). The point is to consider our conformity with Christ in such a way as to see whether we have also deformed him. The point is to stand before the mirror and describe the face reflected there, to see whether it is like the face of Christ—Christ the New Person, Christ the Divine Model—or whether his features and mine are completely unlike. And *deliberately* to keep silent about a grave sin is a matter of great importance, since it means I am lying to myself: I believe I can lie to a God who pierces the interior of a human being, a God who reads my heart. I believe I can deceive God by deceiving the priest who hears my confession.

Sometimes this attitude can be understandable. Human shame at having committed shameful faults can do us a foul turn. But remember, we are not standing before a judge who is listening to our confession in order to sentence us. We are standing before a kind and loving Father, who is awaiting our return as his prodigal son or daughter, in order to robe us in festive garments of the finest as he prepares a great celebration in our honor.

In circumstances like these, to attempt to hide a serious sin out of fear or shame is the most foolish thing imaginable. It means believing that my sin cannot be forgiven by an all-powerful God who is always ready to forget the past.

We might put it this way: In cases like these there is always an unhealthy mixture of despair and pride. We fail to trust in God's goodness, and we puff ourselves up by thinking that our sins are too big for him. Perhaps they *are* great sins. We are not trying to minimize the malice of human beings. But as compared with the least act of Christ—as compared with his least will to redeem us—all the world's sin and all the sins of the world are *nothing at all*. What can we say? His will to save us is signed in his spilled blood!

And so, as we approach the time of our confession, what we need is simplicity, evangelical childlikeness, and the absence of fear or shame. If we have not been ashamed to sin, then neither let us be ashamed to return to the Lord.

3. Did I perform the penance I was given? Did I make reparation for any injury to others? Have I tried to put into practice my resolution to lead a better life in keeping with the Gospel?

The "penance," or "penitential satisfaction," that the priest imposes upon us, or suggests, is calculated to restore us to a situation or state of justice. All sin destroys the equilibrium, the balance, of God's plan for human beings. True, I must perform the penance "the priest gives me."

And so it will be a fine thing if the priest is always a good pastor, an intelligent shepherd, and is able clearly to discern each penitent's particular situation, so that he will assign a penance (= a treatment, a cure) that will restore the sufferer to health. Then the penitent can leave his or her state or moment of vice in the past, and cross over to the opposite virtue which this vice has crushed.

But it will be a very good thing too for each penitent Christian, along with performing the penance the confessor gives, to make a particular judgment of each personal situation so as to be able to "impose" a penance upon himself or herself as well—a "salutary" penance, a curative penance, one that will cure that particular penitent of his or her moral or spiritual evils. Greedy persons will want to make a concrete effort to be generous with their goods. A haughty or prideful person will be inclined to perform concrete works of humility, coming down to the level of others and forming a community of brothers and sisters with them. The gluttonous will deprive themselves of legitimate pleasures of the table, to return to a healthy balance between the legitimate enjoyment of these goods and their forbidden abuse. Persons given to anger, whose temperament frequently betrays them, should examine themselves in the light of the gentleness which Christ proposes to them, and to which he invites them, and should discover, within the limits of their feeble capacities, the concrete opportunities they have for cooperating with the grace to be meek and humble of heart. And so on, through the whole gamut of sins.

There are no "sins in the abstract." Nor are their virtues which stay on the level of the theoretical. We have to come down to factual cases, situations through which we pass every day, in order to see, *right there*, what it is I must convert myself from, and Who it is I must convert myself to. In this way, performing my penance will be a "ratification of my normality." It will mean living in the grace and justice of God.

When the confessor imposes easy penances (generally, prayers of one kind or another), it will be prudent and practicable—after all, we are forgetful—to perform them as soon as possible, so that we shall not have to begin our next confession by saying we "forgot to say our penance." But this is not only prudent and practical, it is also the profound attitude of someone who, with an eager heart, seeks to run the good race again, and fight the good fight.

Many people believe that going to confession simply means telling the priest all the bad things that happened, as one might recount to a friend a play one has seen in a theater. These people "describe" situations—I did this or I did that or I forgot to do this—ending up with "That's all I can remember, Father," or something of the sort.

Let us begin at the beginning. Confession is not a simple telling of my sins (or "mistakes," as we like to say nowadays, so that sinning will be something like making an error in the multiplication tables). True, I have to tell things. But this is not enough. When I tell a priest my sins in confession, I must examine them very closely—not with unhealthy scrupulosity, but with delicacy of conscience—to try to see the reason for my sin, the reason for this stumbling block along the road of salvation.

For example, if, by my sin, I have violated justice, then of course I must repair this breach of justice. If I accuse myself of not paying my employees a just salary (especially if I do not pay them the minimum wage), I cannot accuse myself of not paying a just wage in my next confession all over again, because after my previous confession I had the obligation to remedy the situation—to *restore the justice* that had been "broken" by my "infraction" of justice. If I am unjust in the way I treat my children, or my spouse, or my relatives, it is not enough to tell my confessor about it. The famous old "firm purpose amendment" that we used to read about in our catechisms means that I have to apply a remedy to the situation, so that in my next confession I shall have at least begun to extricate myself from this state of affairs. The "firm purpose of amendment" is the obligation to *repair* the injustices committed, of whatever kind they were. If they consisted of calumny or detraction, I am obliged to make restitution of the reputation I have stolen. If they were acts of theft or fraud, I am obliged to restore the goods I have taken. And so on.

It will not always be easy to be converted. It will not always be easy to put into practice our good intentions to make a change of life according to the Gospel. At no time did our Lord speak of things being "nice and easy." Sometimes it will be easy, and at other times it will be difficult. A thousand things can come in to bog down my conversion, or even push my good intentions back to point zero. It may not be easy. But it is not impossible. It does not even come close to being impossible.

There is an old saying, "When you can't do a little, do a lot." When we see the task as an arduous one, we exert more effort. We bend all the forces of our mind and will to "find a way out." When the gain to be had is small, we do not consider it important, and so our efforts are small too. It is the little things we cannot do. When it is a big thing, we fight till we win.

We must never forget, our Lord does not ask the impossible. "Despite the increase of sin, grace has far surpassed it" (Rm 5:20). God never abandons the just, or leaves them to their fate. The Lord is a God of forgiveness, who "wants none to perish but all to come to repentance" (2 P 3:9). It is God who causes both our will to succeed and our success. It is Christ who bears, today as yesterday, the main burden of our crosses. We cannot take a single step along the road of conversion unless he moves us by his grace to take that step. Then the next steps, too, all of them, are the work of his grace. And finally, the victory of our complete conversion is the true fruit of his grace: it is he who has harvested it, to make a present of it to us.

Naturally, our cooperation is required—our non-opposition to his mighty deed of rescue and redemption. The Ritual asks me if I have "tried to put into practice my resolution to lead a better life." Hell, they say, is paved with good intentions. There is a great deal of truth in this. It is not enough to express our desires, not even the best desires. We must begin to shape the content of those desires in our daily life. Once we are convinced that God came into the world not for the healthy but for the sick, once we realize that there is more joy in heaven on account of one sinner who is converted than for ninety-nine just who have no need of asking forgiveness, once we see in the Gospel that it is we ourselves who are the lost sheep which the Lord goes in search of and carries home on his shoulders, once we recognize ourselves in Zacchaeus, in the woman taken in adultery, and Mary Magdalen at our Lord's feet, once we see that the treason of Judas marks us as traitors too, once Peter's denial slaps us in the face with our own timidity and cowardice, once the insults Jesus has to suffer reveal to us how we have insulted him ourselves, once we really come to grasp how every sin moves the Heart of Jesus to compassion and mercy—then we shall begin to feel capable of amending our lives. Then at last we shall try to make a change, seeing what cause for gladness and peace this change will be, this fruit of the works of the Spirit—just as sorrow and war within us are the "reward" of sin.

"Putting my resolution into practice" means looking for a way to show, in this or that particular deed, that my resolution was genuine, and that therefore the Word of the Gospel is worthy of credit. The Apostles were the "living gospels," the witnesses, relied on by those who had not seen the Lord. but who believed nonetheless. Their faith was not only faith in a word, it was faith in a life style, in a manner of living—faith in a total, integral attitude that makes me *be* this way instead of some other way. Changing my life "in accordance with the Gospel" is nothing but coming to the realization, *by my own experience* of falls (my "disgraces") and graces, that Christ is not *a* way of life, he is *the* way of life—the only really new *way* of life, the only way that has the power to challenge us to an encounter with ourselves, with our brothers and sisters, and with God.

B. Examination According to the Forms Given in the New Ritual

In the light of three great themes of the Word of God, the penitent can make a good review of his or her life. The New Rite of Penance offers us this opportunity. The three themes are, "You shall love the Lord your God with your whole heart," "Love one another as I have loved you," and "Be perfect as your Father is perfect."

Under each of these three great themes, the Church offers us, in the Ritual itself, a rather long series of questions to answer. We shall continue as above—quoting the questions asked in the Ritual, with as brief a consideration on each one as we can have and still make a complete review of our life.

1. The Lord says: "You shall love the Lord your God with your whole heart."

Here we find ourselves back at the First Commandment of God's Law, all summed up in a love that is a response to the love with which God first loved us. Let us see what path the Ritual invites us to follow in its series of questions.

1. Is my heart set on God, so that I really love him above all things and am faithful to his commandments, as a son loves his father? Or am I more concerned about the things of this world? Have I a right intention in what I do?

Here are two questions which we can and should answer.

The vocation of a son or daughter of God is the vocation of someone who has been "converted to God." To be converted to someone means to make everything converge on the one to whom we are being converted. It means to "turn toward." It means to align our course straight toward God, toward the First, toward the Absolute. Our heart can play us many a trick. We can love well, or we can love badly. We can choose what we think is good because it presents itself to us in fine clothing, and yet it is evil. We can deceive ourselves, for we are weak and fallible. Merely wishing to love God does not automatically mean really loving him.

And so the question given in the Ritual reads, "really." In other words, do we love God with a true love, with a love not false, not "falsified"? Do we love him with a love that searches for *him*, knowing that all other things will be given us besides, and forgetting a little the "I" that sometimes becomes such a demanding tyrant?

Here again, the love we are talking about is not just any love, but the highest degree of charity—a "love of benevolence" that can be characterized as that of a daughter or son for his or her father or mother. It is a matter of living "filially"—living in dependence on, and dialogue with, this God we call "Father." And the only person who lives in a relationship with his or her father is the one that dialogues with him, listening to him and speaking to him with complete confidence. A person who fails to listen to his or her father or speak to him is actually treating him as if he had died. So it is with us. We cannot behave with God as if we were orphans.

But notice the question in the Ritual asks whether we are "faithful to his commandments." The essence of a parent-child relationship is rooted in obedience, such as Christ showed toward his Father, becoming obedient to the death, even death on a cross. What is demanded is not a merely intellectual act of faith consisting in the recognition of the existence of a God whom one may call "Father." It is a matter of *living* as a good son or daughter behaves toward his or her most wonderful Father. It is a matter of *putting into practice* the Word of God we hear calling us to "filiation"—calling us to the condition of sons and daughters of God.

This "putting into practice" will enable us to avoid abstractions and theorizing when it comes to Christianity, as if it all consisted in assenting to *ideas* about God. What is important is to allow Christ to prolong his activity in our own history, in the story of our own lives.

And this is something entirely new.

It is *preferential* love for the things of this world that is reprehensible, or blameworthy. Let us note that we are not being asked "not to be concerned" with the things of this world. We are being asked not to be *more* concerned with them. We *have* to be occupied with the things of this world. We are in *this* world, in *this* history, in *this* country, with *these* parents and relatives, and in *these* circumstances. To long for something different would be vain desire and escapism. Let us not practice escapism. But let us dedicate a *preferential* attention to the Kingdom of God. This is what Jesus taught us. *All other things* will be given to us besides, by a God who denies nothing to those who seek him first.

A right scale of values begins with "Number One." Number One is God, and nothing can replace him. But—have we not replaced him on occasion (and on more than one occasion)? Has the Lord not been relegated to our spare time, or to circumstances in which *I had need* of him because things were not going my way? Has not God sometimes come after my family, my goods, my business, my career, my status, my reputation, my trips, my ambitions, my projects? New questions, needing new answers.

All things are good except sin. In the life story of an individual man or woman, however, not all good things are appropriate. We cannot simply opt for all good things, or we shall be left without any. A right act of prudence has to be performed, in order to choose among several good things. And every choice implies a rejection of the alternative not chosen. Keeping in account my vocation, my place in our family, the natural right I have to certain goods in order to have food and shelter, clothing, and an education—keeping in account the services I am obliged to render my neighbor, my cultural duties in view of the talents I have received, and certain healthy inclinations and instincts I may satisfy—keeping in account all these things, perhaps I must place clear limits on my appetites.

There are people who are like a bottomless barrel. Give these persons all the goods on the face of the earth and you will never satisfy them. There will always be something more for them to desire. We can become insatiable. And insatiable persons *always* relegate God to second place, since their time is taken up, and their being is preoccupied, with "things"—realities that are not only less than God, they are less than the human person himself or herself.

And there we have our question. What will be our reply?

The goodness or "badness"—the "malice," as it is called—of our actions is rooted in the *intention* with which I was moved to do this or that. Thus I have an obligation to "rectify my intentions," to educate my intentions—to "purify" my intention, so that it does not make a mistake.

If I do something good in order to glorify God and serve my neighbor, this will enhance the goodness of the action, even if it does not seem all that wonderful a thing in the doing. But if I do something good and my intention is vanity or vainglory—if my desire is to be held of great account, and I merely feign a good intention—then that action, even if it is a good one in itself, will be "vitiated," corrupted, by the depraved intention with which I perform it.

Hence the great importance of delving down to the depths of our being, down where the works to be born are first conceived—down in the "intention zone," where the goodness of the future works can either sprout up or fail and die—and anticipate action *there*. "Have I a right intention"—purity of intention—"in what I do?"

2. *God spoke to us in his Son. Is my faith in God firm and secure? Am I wholehearted in accepting the Church's teaching? Have I been careful to grow in my understanding of the faith, to hear God's word, to listen to instructions on the faith, to avoid dangers to faith? Have I been always strong and fearless in professing my faith in God and the Church? Have I been willing to be known as a Christian in private and public life?*

Nearly all of these questions have to do with faith, and witness to that faith. A Christian is a believer, who has an obligation to give an account of his or her faith. Christians ought to bear witness, following the example of Christ our Model, of the faith they profess by demonstrating it in their works.

The first two questions contain words that will be, or should be, in the answers too: "firm and secure"—"wholehearted." It is not just a matter of some faith or other. It is a matter of a firm, secure, "solid" faith. We are not speaking just of any "acceptance of the Church's teaching" you please. We are speaking of an acceptance that is "wholehearted"— endowed with a certain vigor, a "lively" faith, a faith that escapes the fragility of a human being's responses and becomes the response that Christ makes in each of us.

Each of the questions in this series presupposes the question, "Have we familiarized ourselves with the Word of God—this God who 'has spoken to us through his Son' (Heb 1:2)?" This question is an important one, for faith comes by hearing. Faith has its basis in the hearing of the Word of God who reveals himself to us?

Do we read the Holy Bible frequently, even daily? Do we meditate on it? Does it become the motive force of our actions? We cannot follow or love a God we do not know. We cannot have faith in a God we have not heard. Hence the importance of frequent contact with God's Word. It is this Word that will call forth within us a "wholehearted acceptance" of that very Word, in faith.

But the Word of God has not been sent forth to waft about in thin air. It has been "deposited" in, bestowed upon, the Church of Christ. This is why the faith that springs from God's Word imposes upon us the obligation of knowing and following the "Church's teaching"—that other "word" given us for our guidance, in the light of the Gospel, through all the maze of situations in which we as Christians find ourselves immersed, the political, social, economic, and so on. There is a whole "magisterial corpus," a body of teachings, which the Church, our Mother and Teacher, continuously offers us for our guidance. At the supreme level, this teaching organ is called the "Pontifical magisterium." At the local level, the Church teaches us through the ordinary magisterium of the Bishops. On special occasions, as in Councils, or Synods of Bishops "new" teachings are presented, which we may not only not spurn, but which we are obliged in conscience to accept. Christian bookstores, pamphlet racks, and libraries abound in material which provides that service of charity and work of mercy called "teaching the ignorant"— instructing us in things we are not familiar with but which we ought to know. Do we take advantage of the efforts of so many of our brothers and sisters who have devoted their lives to deepening the faith of the Church (and thereby the faith of each individual one of us)? Are we building a Christian library in our homes, so that our families may take advantage of it to strengthen their faith?

The third question has a negative dimension, which we may not pass over lightly. It says we are "to avoid dangers to the faith." Frankly, this is an area in which we are often lax and foolhardy.

What is enjoined on us here is not to avoid encounters of the faith with non-Catholic or non-Christian positions held by persons of good will who are seeking God in all sincerity. The Ritual is speaking here of doctrines or attitudes that attack, or oppose the faith. The fact that we seek to enter into dialogue with every human being of good will in no way implies that we are converting the Christian faith into a "syncretism," a kind of doctrinal potpourri in which every imaginable teaching somehow becomes good for something. No, many things are true, or are true in some way, but not everything.

Just as in our physical life we flee situations in which we can contract diseases, out of a healthy instinct of self-preservation, so also must we flee another type of disease, much more serious than the ones that call for medicines or doctors—the illnesses of the soul. In matters of faith, in fact in everything which makes for a Christian life, there are "orthodox" attitudes—correct attitudes—and unorthodox attitudes.

But on the other hand, we are not engaging in a "witch hunt"— looking for error where none exists. Nothing could be further from our thoughts. But we are trying to see doctrinal error and evil behavior where they really are, where there are roads our Lord would never have travelled.

There is a kind of popular broad-mindedness that says, "All religions are good." This sort of statement has to be handled very carefully. True, most religions adhere to principles of the natural order, and to a manner of living that is morally correct. But this is not the only thing that is at stake. At stake here are the truth of history, and the full truth of life, according to a salvific model—*the* model proposed to us by Christ—a model he bequeathed to us as the only sure path to salvation. Accordingly, not everything is good—not Jehovah's Witnesses (although they have good things), not the Mormons (although their solidarity with their neighbor is so admirable), not the Seventh Day Adventists (although there are plenty of good Adventists), and not the devotion to Our Lady of Nacedah (in spite of the miracles she may seem to have worked for me).

Have we been careful to "avoid dangers to the faith"?

The last two questions in our second series are directed against a certain cowardice that tends to arise in Christians' hearts—frequently in some, only occasionally in others. The Ritual speaks to us of "strength," "fearlessness," and "willingness to be known as a Christian."

This is an attitude that is not always easy to have. It is not always easy to avoid falling in with the rhythm of the world, where "everything goes." It is not always easy not to care what "people will say." Often enough human shame will be stronger than our capacity for fidelity, and will cause us to topple toward "public opinion" when what we ought to be doing is standing up for our own opinion.

No, it is not always easy. But it is desirable, and it is possible. And it is the only attitude possible for a Christian, for Christ will deny whoever denies him, and will stand up for whoever stands up for him on earth. We must not only not "destroy" our sisters and brothers, we must "edify" them. Often enough, the enemies of Christ and of his Church carry the day not because they have won the battle, but because we have beaten a retreat. Not that we are supposed to turn into crusaders of buckler and sword, warriors who transfer political attitudes (often very doubtful ones) from the world to the Church. The point is not to be always on the attack, in a spirit of "warlikeness," but to demonstrate, in word and work, that we are men and women of faith, men and women of conviction. The point is to defend the House of God and its spiritual goods, just as we would defend our homes and our families.

Evidently, this defense will not be undertaken with the arms with which the things of the world are defended—but with the evangelical arms of truth, goodness, justice, peace, sincerity, a communion of brothers and sisters, and the cross.

Now, there are some "true" weapons for you.

3. Have I prayed morning and evening? When I pray, do I really raise my mind and heart to God or is it a matter of words only? Do I offer God my difficulties, my joys, and my sorrows? Do I turn to God in time of temptation?

The first two questions here concern our prayer life. Prayer implies adoration, thanksgiving, and petition. Do we adore—really adore—the true God, the Almighty, Creator of heaven and earth? Do we acknowledge him as the One who is above all, so that we ascribe to him a unique, absolute place or status? Do we feel a certain admiration for his grandeur and his goodness?

Are we grateful for what he has given us, spiritual and material goods alike, especially faith? Are we grateful to him for having adopted us as his sons and daughters in the maternal bosom of the communion of the Church?

Do we "petition" him as a poor person begs a favor—unconditionally? Or better yet, conditioned on whether what we ask be his will? Sometimes a false pride inclines us to say that we do not want to ask God for anything—we do not want to be one of those people who are "always asking for something." This is consummate foolishness. What is to be avoided is not to ask badly. We must ask well. And asking well means asking for "true favors," not "false favors." "False favors" are evils, couched in phraseology that makes them sound like something good.

Not only *may* we ask God for things, then. We *must* ask God for things. When we ask God for something we are performing an act of humility. We realize that we cannot do everything by our own means—with our personal resources. And so we ask God for these things. We are also performing an act of hope: we have trust and confidence that we shall receive what we ask.

But do we ask him for "true favors"? Do we not sometimes ask him for vain, unnecessary things? Do we ask him for an increase of faith, hope, and charity? Do we ask him for favors for our brothers and sisters? Do we ask him for the conversion of sinners? Do we ask him for the reconciliation of enemies? Do we ask him to help those who seek him and yet do not believe in him? Are we not impatient in our petitions, and leave off making them when it seems to us that God has not answered us within twenty-four hours?

Let us not forget that, even though our Lord knows our needs, he has conditioned the bestowal of his favors on prayer. More than once, Christians have been known to limit their prayer to the prayer of petition—and in moments of anguish, at that, when they find themselves in dire economic straits, or when some special problem overwhelms them. No, prayer ought to be our daily bread, in good times as in bad, in joy as in pain, like the prayer of our Lord and the saints. We have an ancient custom of praying in the morning and in the evening, to commend to God the day that is just beginning and to thank him for the day that is ended. Do we do that? Every day? And is it a dialogue, in which we listen for our Lord, and answer him—or is it simply a monologue, in which *I* lift my voice of noisy praise, or petition, as if there were no one else there (the more important one!)? Is my prayer something I merely perform exteriorly, a set of stereotyped motions I go through, a routine, a duty, so that I do not know why, for what, and to whom I am praying? Prayer is not just a matter of praying. It is doing so in such a way as to become a praying *person*.

We have been speaking of prayer in the strict sense of the word. But of course our whole life can be a "prayer," too, in the sense of an offering presented to God. Many things happen to me every day that can be offered to him in this way—besides being made the subject of prayer in the strict sense of the word (prayer as we have been discussing it up to now). There is no day without its "difficulties, joys, and sorrows."

How do I handle these life situations? How do I relate these events, these happenings, to the explicit or permissive will of God? (Some things that happen to me are willed by God absolutely; others, the evil things that happen, are only permitted by him). Have I made them an "offering" to God—something I can deliver over to God as a genuine redemptive sacrifice?

The last question is about temptation. This is a subject fraught with difficulties. Many a penitent has accused himself or herself in confession of having had "temptations." And that is all. Just temptations.

But what does that mean? Does "having temptations" mean I have actually committed a fault against charity or justice toward my neighbor? Or does it mean I merely *felt* like shirking my duties and allowing myself to be overcome by sloth?

In order to commit sin, and incur guilt, one must not only be tempted, one must actually fall. In the Our Father, when we ask God not to lead us into temptation, we do not mean, "Keep us from having any temptations,'' but "Do not allow us to *succumb* to temptation''—to *actually fall into sin* as a result of our temptations. Bad thoughts are, of themselves, only temptations. If I have not sought them, or expressly consented to them, they are not sins. Evil desires, unsought, are not sins. They are nothing, either before my conscience or before God. Let me repeat: One often hears in confession, "Father, I accuse myself of having a bad thought, which I put out of my mind right away." And I have to answer: "I am very glad. This is not something to accuse yourself of, it is something to praise God for, and thank him for. You did exactly what you are supposed to do." A temptation resisted is a victory.

But at the same time we must face the fact that temptations, those works of the Devil, do roam about seeking to make us fall. Our Lord asks us to be watchful and to pray, so that we will not fall. He asks us not to be smug. People who think they stand on the heights—even if they really do—can be suddenly cast down from those heights. Scripture asks us not to be foolhardy, not to be like those who love danger and end by smashing themselves to pieces, victims of their own insane suicide. Our Lord asks us to bear up under the struggle, for no one is tempted beyond his or her own strength.

But then of course we have an obligation to build up our "own strength." If I have done nothing on my side, if I do not lead a Christian life, if I do not pray, do not go to Mass, do not practice frequent confession—if I do not try, consciously and reflectively, to discover the ways of the Lord, the paths God wishes to lead me in—if I do not devote myself to my neighbor—then it will be a "miracle" indeed if I do not fall.

And so when considering the subject of temptation, we must ask ourselves first of all whether we have gone to our Lord, our Lady, and the Saints to ask for strength to stand firm in the faith—whether we have made use of the adequate natural and supernatural means to fortify ourselves and to persevere in the Christian life.

So there are some more questions. We should be laying some answers on the table.

4. Have I love and reverence for God's name? Have I offended him in blasphemy, swearing falsely, or taking his name in vain? Have I shown disrespect for the Blessed Virgin Mary and the saints?

These questions concern certain acts that are offensive to God or to the saints, and which fall into the category of irreverence or false swearing.

True, certain "curse words" are often merely what we call "materially" irreverent, and actually represent deficiencies in our upbringing more than they do serious blasphemy. But considering the Object of this irreverence, we and our neighbors have a duty to correct these deficiencies of upbringing, and root out the detestable habit of taking the name of the Lord in vain. After all, we are not even supposed to insult our equals; how much deeper and higher a reason we have for not insulting One who is higher and greater than all creation put together—and who has done so little to merit our insults!

The Church is merciful, and appreciates the fact that there are times when certain attitudes of ours are the fruit not so much of an evil heart, but of the despair and suffering that can so often estrange us from God. But once the moment of pain has passed, once we have begun to regain control of ourselves, the moment has come to identify our problem and solve it *correctly*. That is, the time has come to solve it not by launching the broadsides of my fury or my desperation against Him who should be precisely my peace and consolation, but in some reasonable, humanly responsible way instead.

As for the casual expression in which God is called as witness to this or that—"By God, this," or "By God, that," the majority of times they are just thoughtless. Of course, there are also those occasions on which the oath, ". . . so help me God," has become legitimated by use, as when it is pronounced in a courtroom, or upon inauguration into a public office. (It is to be regretted, however, that its use is so widely received in this latter case, where, because of human weakness and malice, we would really have to say that it is rather foolhardy for a public official to take God to witness that he or she is going to discharge the duties of that office honestly.) God has no wish to be made responsible for every casual remark we may feel like making. If what we say is true, it is true, and our hearers should be able to believe it on my word.

If my word is not good, then neither is my oath "by God."

5. Do I keep Sundays and feast days holy by taking a full part, with attention and devotion, in the liturgy, and especially in the Mass? Have I fulfilled the obligation of going to confession when needed and the precept of going to communion during the Easter season?

Sunday is the "Lord's Day." Just what is the "Lord's Day"?
The Lord's Day is simply the celebration of the Resurrection of
Christ, week after week. In ancient times it was called, "Weekly Easter." It was the first feast day the Church ever had. The Christian
assembly would gather together around the Word of God, the Sacrifice,
and the Eucharistic Banquet, to celebrate Life's triumph over death. In
the Gospels we read that Jesus rose "on the first day of the week" (Lk
24:1)—that is, on Sunday. From earliest times Christ's followers considered this day something very special, something deserving of their
honor, by reason of the One who was being celebrated on this day—by
reason of the Paschal Mystery accomplished in the humanity of Christ
and promised to all his members, the Church.

These very brief considerations can provide the background for the
following questions: What is Sunday for us? What meaning does it have
for me that I gather with my family in a church and recall and relive the
Passover of Jesus Christ? True, *I am obliged* to assist at Sunday Mass, but
. . . is there not an obligation of love, too, that comes before the canonical
obligation—an obligation dictated by the laws of the heart, and by the
commitment of a mind that *believes* (a way of *knowing*) in Christ, the
Glorious One, the Cause of all faith, and all future resurrection?

Have we not, instead, often considered liturgical celebrations as a
kind of insupportable burden, which the Church (or the hierarchy, for we
are accustomed to define the "Church" as our official leaders, even
though they only form part of the Church) lays upon our weary shoulders?

But do we not celebrate people's birthdays, and other "happy an-
niversaries"? And does it not give us great joy to do so? And does it not
give us pleasure to gather together with friends, even when that is all there
is to it—meeting our friends? The part the Church asks us to play on
"Sundays and feast days" is a "full part." We are being asked for
action. We are being asked to do everything we can to emerge from a
passivity which would make us pure "receivers" in the liturgy, as if we
were watching a film on television, and become *actors* in the drama. We
are asked to perform our role "with attention and devotion," for we are
entering upon a great moment of prayer. We are entering upon the
greatest of the acts of Christ and his Church—the act that signifies, and
causes, our salvation. Our "attention and devotion" will not be just the

attention and devotion of one who is listening to what is going on, so as not to miss anything in the Readings, or anything Father has to say in the "sermon." We are not attending a class or lecture. We are *living a celebration*, and this celebration is a *festival*, in every way.

The liturgy of the Church offers us a grand occasion for celebration. How do I celebrate it? Half asleep? Do I arrive late for Mass? Am I there unwillingly? Do I fail to prepare myself adequately? Do I participate "unconsciously," unaware of what is taking place? Am I so annoyed with the people around me, great individualist that I am, that I fail to participate as part of the community?

Often we hear people say: "Father, I like the church when it's empty. I go in often when there's nobody there, and pray." And I tell them: "I'm glad you go into church and pray. I don't care whether it's empty or full." Of course, when it is a matter of private, personal devotion, as when I am making a visit to the Blessed Sacrament for example, whether there is "anybody there" or not is a matter of taste. But the liturgy of the Church is an action that is *public*, communitarian, and I am expected to express my *social* religious side there. To pray without anyone around is one thing. To pray in the company of my sisters and brothers is another. Both forms should be cultivated, without depreciating either. I *should* pray alone, and I *should* pray in the company of others. In liturgical celebrations—and in a special way in the Sunday Eucharist—I join with the rest of the Church to celebrate, as Church, the victory of the Lord. I am celebrating the One who is "Lord" precisely because he holds dominion over Death, so that Death no longer has dominion over him. I join with an ordained assembly, presided over by the Bishop, or by a priest, who stands in the place of Christ. I unite myself to this great act of faith, hope, and charity. I join with my neighbor in petition and thanks-giving. I enter into communion with the Body and Blood of Christ, as a true worshiper in Spirit and in truth.

Have I thought about all this? Am I familiar with the prayers of the Mass, so that I can pray them in a spirit of celebration, either by singing them or reciting them along with the others?

The Church prescribes that its sons and daughters confess when necessary and receive Communion *at least once a year*, during the Easter season. But this is a *minimum*. This is prescribed in view of the weakness or negligence of those who are estranged from the Church, and who never take conscious part in the life of that Church—that new People of God and Mystical Body of Christ made up of all the baptized. But this minimum has never been proposed *as an ideal*. Quite the contrary, it is the lowest step on the ladder, the beginner's step, to be followed by others, under penalty of remaining in our indigence and need. But it is true that the obligation itself is formulated in terms of this minimum.

If I rest content with this minimum, without doing more, there is no doubt I shall be impoverished. The Christian life does not aim for the minimum. It aims for the optimum, for the most. A good Christian does not choose minimums. A good Christian "goes for the whole thing."

And we ourselves—how do we go about it? Do we begin by asking ourselves when it was that we last went to confession? Do we recall whether we prepared for that confession well, by examining our conscience according to the criteria of the Gospel? If it has been quite some time since my last confession, do I easily recall what has happened since, even though it has been so many months now? Have I not been procrastinating when it comes to genuine repentance? Since my last confession, have I lived in God's grace? Did my last confession result in my living "in grace, or in disgrace"? That is, did I make a "good confession"? It very frequently happens that those who celebrate the Sacrament of Reconciliation at frequent intervals not only have good memories, but a "right" memory, as well—they have what is called "delicacy of conscience." Those, on the other hand, who confess only from time to time, or once a year, seem to remember nothing. They have nothing of which to accuse themselves, and eventually come to have "lax consciences," so that even the most elementary notion of sin has disappeared for them.

Let us neither be lax, nor "scrupulous." Let us shape and mold our spirit "according to that of Christ Jesus," in order to be like him. The observance of the precepts of the Church is not the task of minors, or of people with a servile mentality. Let us observe them as sons and daughters. This is the best definition of what we are: sons and daughters of a God we call Father.

6. Are there false gods that I worship by giving them greater attention and deeper trust than I give to God: money, superstition, spiritism, or other occult practices?

"Worshipping false gods," in the sense of this question, does not mean belonging to another religion. This question is addressed to Catholics. What should "God" mean for us? Should God not be the greatest thing there is, the motive of my absolute confidence, the "place" I stand that gives me strength and support, the main motive of my life and all my acts?

Among the other possible "goods" I may have is wealth, with all the preoccupations of gaining it and keeping it. We pursue wealth for "security." But for a believer, security is God and his Word. All else beside is elusive and perishable. A certain amount of material goods and money is necessary. No one can doubt that. The point is, they should not be my reason for living. I remove God from his rightful place, a place I should zealously reverence and respect, and I put wealth there—a little god with a little *g* and feet of clay—as transitory, as perishable, as evanescent as any idol that ever existed.

Is this my own situation? Have I an inordinate desire to become rich? Am I satisfied with what I have? If I aspire to have more, are my aspirations "ordinate," moderate, appropriate, within reason? Do I correctly "relativize" the goods of earth, knowing that I am more than my riches and that God is more than I and my riches together?

The next example the Ritual gives of a "false god" is superstition. There are people who, instead of placing their confidence in our Lord, place it in their horoscope as it appears in the daily paper. They place their confidence in how Saturn is getting along with Venus these days. Some even believe in fortune-telling, or in clairvoyants who foretell ruined marriages and other misfortunes, or in people who assure you "scientifically" (too bad for science, then!) that we can communicate with the souls of the departed, or in whatever magician of this type happens along at the moment, regardless of the absurdity of their proposals or solutions for the problems of life. More than one of these charlatans actually advertises in the newspapers, announcing office hours, "Monday through Friday, at such and such hours, at such and such an address," and assuring their prospective clients of the "supernatural powers" of the person who will deign to receive us.

But they would not exist if there were not people who trust them. Am I one? Or do I seriously trust my horoscope? Have I descended to the level of those who will exchange gold for brass? Once more—idolatry does not consist solely in formal adoration of other actual gods who are considered to be God. There are many false gods seeking to occupy the place of the one true God we call "Lord."

Let us consider these questions carefully, and let us keep in mind the Lord's commandment: "You shall not have other gods besides me."

2. The Lord says: "Love one another as I have loved you."

This is the second commandment, and it is similar to the first. As we know, it is impossible to love God without loving our brothers and sisters, and a person who says he or she loves God without loving his or her neighbor is a liar, according to the words of St. John.

Let us see, then, what questions the Ritual will ask, in the section on the Rite of Penance, to help us make a good examination of conscience regarding our love of neighbor—our sister and brother.

1. Have I a genuine love for my neighbors? Or do I use them for my own ends, or do to them what I would not want done to myself? Have I given grave scandal by my words or actions?

There are times when we think we love others, when in reality our relationship with them is nothing but self-seeking. We think we are loving someone, when actually we only have an inordinate desire to be held in account and be loved ourselves.

Our neighbor has the right to expect from us Christians not just some love or other, but love with a qualifier: we are to love one another *as Christ loved us*. Let us consider whether in dealing with our brothers and sisters we have not perhaps seriously failed in justice and charity in their regard, applying a "double standard" in our relationships: strict justice, heaped up and overflowing, for ourselves, and justice in a broad, loose sense—a stingy justice—for others. Have we followed the "Golden Rule"—to do unto others as we would have others do unto us, and to do what we would not have them do? Or on the contrary, have I uttered a cry that would pierce the heavens when someone has offended me, or when I have not been understood, when all the while I have not understood others or been the least concerned with my offenses against them? It is one thing to enter into a relationship with another person considering him or her as my equal, someone with the same rights as I have, a human being deserving of my consideration and attention, a son or daughter of

God whom I look upon as the object of my tender and delicate love—and another thing altogether to treat my neighbor as an object of use and utility, so that if this person serves me, I appreciate him or her, and if not, he or she is to be discarded.

Persons are not things. Even things are to be handled with care. How much more our neighbors, our sisters and brothers in Christ himself! They are immeasurably more deserving of our attention and concern. How important it is to avoid all abuse of persons, lest I put myself in the position of being their proprietor, when in actuality my vocation is to be the servant of God and of human beings.

There is a passage in the Gospels in which our Lord Jesus Christ places us on our guard against those who scandalize any of his little children. He says it would be better for such a person to have a millstone tied about his or her neck and be drowned in the depths of the sea. It is a powerful image. To "scandalize" a brother or a sister means to pervert his or her vocation, or to place it in danger by giving bad example.

Let us think long and seriously about what the vocation of a Christian means, both with respect to ourselves and with respect to others. We were born to be followers of Christ. We were born to listen to our Lord, and put his Word into practice. We were born to imitate him, and thus to reshape in ourselves the image and likeness of God our Father and of the New Creation which is Christ. We were born to help all creation to return to God, to enter into God's glory. We were born so that, if it were possible, all humanity should be Church, should be the communion of those redeemed by the Blood of Jesus. We Christians are all of this.

Now, what happens when this vocation is distorted, blurred? What happens when we fall away from the call to sanctity, when we seek to serve two masters, when like the bad thief we are unwilling to have Christ "steal" our soul, even at the last hour?

This is the true "scandal." Now the great, howling din arises, that drowns out the symphony God has sought to strike up with us. Now that Voice resounds no more, and the strident shrieks of scandal fill the air in its place. Let us "read our consciences." Let us see whether our word and our conduct have not been the reason for more than one of our brothers' or sisters' falling away from the faith, or not drawing near to it. Let us consider whether our words, and the model of our lives, have not sometimes been the very antithesis of what Christ came to show the world, when he revealed himself to us as the Way.

2. In my family life, have I contributed to the well-being and happiness of the rest of the family by patience and genuine love? Have I been obedient to parents, showing them proper respect and giving them help in their spiritual and material needs? Have I been careful to give a Christian upbringing to my children, and to help them by good example and by exercising authority as a parent? Have I been faithful to my husband (wife) in my heart and in my relations with others?

All these questions concern family duties that are incumbent upon everyone. Let us see what conclusions we can draw from them.

The only way to live a human and Christian life is to live it in peace and gladness. To be the cause of another's sorrow is neither human nor Christian. Joy and peace are the twin causes of good, of fidelity, of grace. "No man is an island." We cannot live in isolation from one another. We cannot be content with "not fighting with anyone." (This can be a great convenience!) We must be involved with others—not with the indiscretion of one who trespasses on private property, but as one who, out of love, takes an interest in other persons, and refuses to be indifferent to the lot of his or her brothers and sisters.

How am I managing to answer these questions? Are my words bitter or cutting? Do I always defend myself when I am offered correction by others? Do I always have to be in the right? When others are right, do I promptly admit it, and correct my own opinions when necessary? Am I impatient with my neighbors' defects, and at the same time eager to have them overlook mine? Have I not sometimes been too proud to admit I was wrong, even when I knew I was?

Jesus showed obedience not only to his parents, but to the civil authorities, provided they did not violate the Law of God. Very frequently, with young people especially, there is a great lack of respect and consideration for parents. The sullen responses, the disobedience, seem to parents to be something that just has to be sadly put up with.

Obedience to parents is a sign of "filiation"—the condition of sons and daughters. "Filial piety," as it is called—dutifulness toward our parents—should be accompanied by a respect which is demonstrated in submission to our parents' authority, as shown by the example of Christ.

Obedience, assistance, and respect will be the true mark of my "filiation." A birth certificate that says that I am the daughter or the son of so-and-so will not suffice. This is mere blood and paper. A son or daughter *in actual fact* is one who behaves as such. Whoever does not act as a son or daughter, is not. Life is not a matter of beautiful theories about duty. Life is a matter of *practice*. Only deeds will prove the authenticity and veracity of my words.

Am I a true son or daughter? Are my attitudes and acts "filial," or are they actually contrary to filiation?

Similarly, to be a parent does not consist merely in having procreated a son or daughter. This is just the beginning. But if I am at my child's side while he or she is growing up, if I indeed bring him or her up properly, along the paths that lead to Christian maturity, then I have fulfilled the commitment of blood and baptism. Now I have expressed, in a clear manner, that I will not abandon my child, that I will continue to be at that child's side even, at times, against his or her will.

Have I not sometimes let the reins of parental authority fall from my hands, under the facile pretext that "times have changed," or that "these are difficult years," or that young people "aren't what they used to be"? Have I not occasionally given my children bad example, and then been over-strict with them in the same matter? This can be exasperating for them!

We are talking about parental *authority*. Is there this authority in our homes? Do we not try to make up for its lack by shouting and waving? But of course we are talking about *parental* authority—fruitful, productive authority, such as only a parent knows how to exercise. Police authority ought to be exercised by a police officer. The authority of a "boss" ought to be exercised by an employer, in accordance with regulations in effect for dealings with employees. A parent should exercise only parental authority.

Now, where is there a parent who is a perfect model of all this? There is only one: the Parent par excellence, God the Father, whom we ought to know, imitate, and cause to be imitated.

In my marital relations, have I sought our mutual good in our living together? Have I sought an unfeigned peace, based on truth and faithfulness? One of the Readings in the Rite of Marriage compares marriage and its relationship with the relationship of Christ with his Church, with the husband called upon to imitate Christ the Bridegroom and the wife to imitate the Church, the Bride of Christ. My conjugal love and mutual service should be like the love and readiness to serve that Christ shows his Church. This may seem a very high model to follow—one impossible to imitate. And yet . . . this is the model proposed for our imitation.

Have I always been faithful to my spouse, in thought and in deed? Have I wounded him or her by ugly words, indifference, or derision? Have I criticized my spouse in front of our children, thus causing him or her to lose respect and authority? Have I duly appreciated the efforts and sacrifices of my spouse for the good of the family? Have I shown him or her those attentions and delicacies that make for a joyous community of life? Have I placed more value in things away from home, and enjoyed them more, than the things I have at home?

Have I threatened or abused my spouse? Have I honored my wife as my friend and mother, or my husband as friend and father? Have I been unfair with my spouse's family, thus wounding our affection for each other and occasioning conflicts, so that it is more difficult now to "get along"? Have I appreciated our common parenthood, or have I sometimes regretted having conceived another child? Have I avoided having children?

Have I spoken disrespectfully of my spouse before others, and complained of his or her defects? Have I prayed for my spouse? Have I prevented my spouse from fulfilling his or her religious duties? Have I been suspicious or jealous? Have I looked at another woman (or another man) without purity of heart?

Have we dealt with each other as children of the same Father? Have we cultivated our faith together?

3. Do I share my possessions with the less fortunate? Do I do my best to help the victims of oppression, misfortune, and poverty? Or do I look down on my neighbor, especially the poor, the sick, the elderly, strangers, and people of other races?

We have already spoken of the right we all have to a certain amount of material things in order to live with dignity and to fulfill our vocation. We saw this when treating of wealth and money. But we also know that in a family, goods are held in common.

In the family of God, we cannot allow some members to be hungry while others are lolling in luxury. Further: we know that, in case of extreme necessity, a person in need has the right to take what he or she needs. Accordingly, for that person, goods are common property, and he or she has the right to have access to them. Here we must examine our use of, and attitude toward, the material goods we have at our disposition.

Do we share these goods? Is there a community, a sharing, of my goods? Have I been concerned systematically to aid those who are less well off than I am? Have I made provision for a monthly budget of expenditures for the needy, with concrete priorities as to who will receive my assistance? Have I not closed myself up within my ivory tower, secure and comfortable, and closed my eyes to what is going on outside? Have I not felt annoyed when having to "listen to somebody's tale of woe"? Have I not felt like "getting out of there as fast as I could"?

What about my spiritual and cultural possessions? Have I shared them with others? Have I performed the work of mercy called "instructing the ignorant"? Do I set aside a part of my time (which is one of my "possessions") to share with those who have need of it? Have I shown appreciation for all my sisters and brothers, without what is called "acceptance of persons," or "human respect"? Or have I looked down on some of them instead, out of a feeling of superiority—failing to consider that, if I am indeed superior to them in any way, I only have more obligations than rights in their regard?

Have conflicts that may have arisen in my country, or the civil or foreign wars of other nations, occasioned my hatred or contempt for other peoples or nations? Have I felt an aversion for "hayseeds" (or "city slickers"), for no better reason than my stupid prejudices? Do I feel a revulsion for members of other races or religions (especially blacks or Jews), oblivious of the fact that every human being is my brother or sister, denying them the opportunity to prove themselves, just because "everybody else" thinks the same as I?

Let us not forget, everything we have said so far on Question Three has to do with the commandment of charity. And let us not think that a "fault against charity" always means that I simply became annoyed with someone over some little thing. It can refer to deep-rooted attitudes and habits I have that I have no intention of overcoming. Here, justice enters into the picture—justice, the forgotten virtue. I am not to do to others what I would not have them do to me. Rather I am to "do unto others as I would have others do unto me." How would *I* wish to be treated if I were poor, or sick, or elderly, or a stranger, or a member of another race? How did Christ treat poor people?

4. Does my life reflect the mission I received in confirmation? Do I share in the apostolic and charitable works of the Church and in the life of my parish? Have I helped to meet the needs of the Church and of the world and prayed for them: for unity in the Church, for the spread of the Gospel among the nations, for peace and justice, etc.?

The Sacrament of Confirmation reaffirmed the new being I received in baptism. My condition of son or daughter of God and witness of our Lord Jesus Christ was ratified. I was anointed to be another Christ in history—my history—doing the works of salvation which Christ began in his history. My life was launched toward a mission—the vocation I had gratuitously received in my baptism. Is there a consistency between my life and my mission?

The Church is an organized hierarchical society, a people presided over and governed by the Pope and the bishops, with the collaboration of the priests and deacons. Nor is it made up only of religious brothers and sisters, who have consecrated themselves to God by making public vows of religion. The Church is the Mystical Body of Christ, made up of all who have been reborn of water and the Spirit in the Sacrament of Baptism.

Accordingly, I am a sharer in the Church's mission: to preach the Gospel of Christ to all men and women, inviting them to live in the Church of the Lord. Consequently, my participation in the works of apostolic charity is not only my right (no one may keep me from it), it is my duty (as a Christian, I may not omit it). The manner of its exercise is manifold, according to the condition and obligations of each one's state of life. But no one may excuse himself or herself from this grand and glorious task of propagating the Gospel, so that it may become the life of the world and life for the world.

There is a *hyper*critical spirit we have, that, with surprising consistency, and incredible casualness, inclines us to pass judgment on the Church. And we are speaking of Catholics—not those who do not belong to the Church or do not believe in Christ. The Church has need of our aid and assistance. The Church needs our prayers, our loyalty, our talents, our time, and our money. The Diocese needs me, as a professional person, or as a salaried worker, as a learned person, or as one with relatively little education. No one can say: ''I have nothing to contribute to the work of evangelization.'' Some teach theology, others do fund-raising. Some visit the sick, others teach religion to children. Some are extraordinary ministers of the Eucharist or have other ministerial functions, others are directors of Christian groups in their places of employment. Some study the Word of God, others work as missioners in places where missionary work is needed. Some are ''Defenders of the Bond'' in ecclesiastical Marriage Tribunals, others care for sick children in hospitals. Some are good at work with youth, others direct priests' retreats. Still others do the cooking for the retreats.

It would be impossible to list all the things that can be done for the sake of the Gospel *in concrete, actually possible tasks*. It is but a matter of discovering what we are good at, and then, once we have discovered what it is, placing ourselves at the service of our sisters and brothers. Christ's Church has need of its sons and daughters. Have I offered my help?

How much help have I offered? Have I been efficient, or, instead ''deficient,'' in actually doing what I have offered to do? Or have I simply failed to respond to requests for help? Have I tended to look down on people who are ''always puttering around the church'' or other Catholic centers? Do I feel a sense of solidarity with those who toil for the upbuilding of the Kingdom in the works of the apostolate? Have I prayed for religious and priestly vocations, and for an increase in the number and dedication of laypersons committed to the task of evangelization? Have I been concerned for the unity of the Church—for the conversion of the ''separated brothers and sisters'' into ''united brothers and sisters''? Have I sabotaged the process of restoration of full communion of all Christians in the Church by my inopportune or unjust criticism? Do I feel the scandal of the disunion among those who profess the same Lord as a wound in my own flesh, seeing that I am a member of Christ's Body?

Let us go over the questions once more . . . let us think about them . . . let us give answers.

5. Am I concerned for the good and prosperity of the human community in which I live, or do I spend my life caring only for myself? Do I share to the best of my ability in the work of promoting justice, morality, harmony, and love in human relations? Have I done my duty as a citizen? Have I paid my taxes?

Let us not think that, since our true country is in heaven, and our citizenship on high, we can therefore neglect our duties and obligations down here on earth. The very opposite is the case. It is precisely by our works of justice and charity *here* that we shall prophetically anticipate the future *there*, in the world beyond. No other view is worthy of credit.

I live in a human community. I live in a nation, a city or township, a neighborhood, and a home. My first neighbor, then—without excluding any human being on the face of the earth, of course—will be my fellow citizens, the people in my neighborhood and town, my fellow workers, the members of my family. The "good and prosperity" spoken of in the Ritual are not something just theoretical. They are something real, and meant for my whole country, city, and neighborhood.

The "good and prosperity" will not come about all by themselves. Who is to bring them about? Public agencies have an obligation, this is true. But theirs is not the only obligation. To expect government to do everything is a kind of cancer. It is a mentality that transforms us into irresponsible minors, children who expect to be spoon-fed, without their contributing anything themselves. This does not absolve government from the efficient discharge of its duties. But we may not be allowed to abdicate our own individuality either, or our own personal, inalienable obligations, with the magic words, "The government should be doing that." Often this is just a subterfuge for the safeguarding of my own selfish interests. Have I been guilty of this subterfuge?

The questions in the Ritual call for "justice" and "morality." This does not necessarily call for embarking on ambitious campaigns or founding organizations. I can promote justice as a high school or college student, and not lose a moment in doing so—simply by applying myself to my studies, so that my teachers and administrators will not have to watch their efforts go "down the drain," and so that my parents' sacrifices will not have been in vain. Isn't this justice? Is it not an injustice to waste time—time which once lost will never return, time of which I must one day give an accounting? Is it not an injustice to permit my teachers to give me their all, and then have to watch me squander it? Is it not an injustice when I allow my elders to pay for my educations and support me during a goodly portion of my life, and not "pay them back"? What I ought to be "paying" them, of course, is the fulfillment of the duties of my state of life.

We have a habit of viewing dishonest ways of behaving as being somehow "OK" just because "everybody does it"—as if our indifference, or insensitivity, or numb inability to react, somehow made them honest. There we sit, at our ease, in a kind of "spiritual easy chair," and nobody is going to make us get out of it. Don't bother me, I'm resting.

When there is a flu epidemic, people take their shots. If a pipe bursts in the house and water is spewing all over the place, I call the plumber. If the TV goes "on the blink," we've packed it off to the repair shop before we think twice. (I'm going to miss my favorite program!) But how do we react when the disease is the one called "bad habits"? When the "epidemic" consists of bad television programs or "dishonest" movies—not pornographic movies, just dumb ones, the kind where your brain gets numb from lack of use—how do we react to *that* kind of threat to our health? Do we take group action? Do we take *any* action?

How do we deal with our personal habits of dishonesty? How do we deal with our family's habits of dishonesty? Have I not perhaps occasionally "slipped somebody a little something on the side" to make things "go a little more smoothly," or so I would not have to pay a traffic fine? What kind of "morality" do you call that?

And what about what the Ritual calls "harmony"? Are we not sowers of discord, disharmony, when we peddle that little bit of gossip that detracts from someone's reputation? Do we not like to wag our tongues a bit over something somebody did, or "the way he is," or "the kind of person she is"? Let us try to think how many times we have pronounced unfavorable judgments on persons or situations within the last month—and how often, within the same length of time, we have spoken well of others.

As for paying taxes, it would be better not to bring this up at all.

Everybody knows you do not have to declare *everything*, because the government knows there is tax evasion going on, and raises the rate to cover it.

Is this true?

If it is, then we are admitting that what we are talking about is tax *evasion*—fraud. And then . . . well, who started the vicious circle, the government, by raising the rate, or individuals, by defrauding the government?

Here is the general rule: A Christian is obligated to obey just laws. True, someone may judge that a law is unjust, and then he or she is no longer obliged in conscience to obey it. But in order to arrive at this conclusion, a person has to have made a serious prudential judgment, and must be able to give an account of the reasons which have led him or her to this behavior. He or she must *prove* that the law is unjust. And until this is done, the law must be obeyed. Not to obey it is a failure in justice, a failure to contribute to the common good of one's country, state, or city.

6. *In my work or profession am I just, hard-working, honest, serving society out of love for others? Have I paid a fair wage to my employees? Have I been faithful to my promises and contracts?*

Do I come on time for work? Do I do my work with competency and efficiency? Am I careful to put in a full day's work, so as not to steal from my employer? Do I consider the fulfillment of my duties at work as a service I owe society? There can be no doubt that I have a right to just renumeration for my services—one that will permit me to live with dignity, care for my family and bring them up properly, and live a well-ordered life. But have I also been conscious of *my* duty to do a responsible job in order to be happy in my work, and to make others happy? Have I offered my work to God, by doing it with love and joy? Or have I bitterly plodded through it as an inescapable burden? Have I been unreliable? Have I been careless about fulfilling my employer's commitments to clients, thereby leaving those clients dissatisfied with my employer?

When someone engages the services of another, he or she is bound to pay that other a *just* wage. A just wage will not always be the one provided by law. Sometimes the minumum wage is an unjust wage. When the minimum wage is unjustly low for *this* person in *this* job, but we think we cannot or should not pay more than the minimum wage, then a just solution must be found for this problem.

Then there are those who do not even pay the minimum wage. Are we by any chance among them? Further: there are labor laws in this country, calculated to provide salaried employees with a minimum of family security. There are maternity benefits. There are retirement benefits. And so there are employers who like to hire bachelors and single women. Why? Because married people "make for too many complications." You have to pay them a salary that will support their whole family. Married women are even worse—they may become pregnant, then you will have to give them time off before and after the baby arrives . . . not to mention family benefits for children from then on.

Apparently we think that some people work, and other people start families and have children. Is this my attitude? Should it not be just the opposite? Should I not prefer to hire someone who is married, precisely because he or she has more need and more obligations than someone who is single? Should I not prefer to hire someone with children rather than someone without them, for the same reason? Have we not put economic problems ahead of human ones? What would be the effect of a habitual attitude like this? Do we not criticize Marxists and "communists" for the outrage of ignoring human problems—for being "inhumane"? Are we not falling into the same failings as we criticize in them?

Employees' benefits are a way of sharing profits. Let us think of a *just* wage rather than of the *minimum* wage. To be just, a wage must be adequate to permit the employee to support his or her family in their normal needs. The fact that another family member may also have a job does not necessarily make any difference. These others, especially the older children of the family, have a right to begin to make their own way, so as to become economically independent enough to start a family of their own.

"Have I been faithful to my promises and contracts?" Is my signature worth anything? Is my word worth anything? The answer I must give to this question about my conduct will say something about the evaluation people will have the right to make about me as a person.

7. Have I obeyed legitimate authority and given it due respect?

It is often with a great deal of levity and thoughtlessness that we pass judgment on those in authority. We easily say that this one or that one is a "crook." But is he or she really? More often than not, our criticism is unfounded—that is, it is founded on the prattle we hear at work or at the grocery store—and it tends to place those who hold any public office in a very bad light.

Have we ever really considered how difficult it is to serve others in public office? Have we thought about the pressures they are under, and the obstacles they encounter in the exercise of their tasks? Have we taken account of how much our unfavorable criticism can undermine the trust of our hearers—in particular the young, who may mold a skeptical mentality with respect to the various governments, local, state, and federal, and turn into everlasting malcontents? Some of the fun we poke at the authorities—is not some of it a sign of real disrespect for the dignity of their office? Justice and respect for our fellow human beings demand our respect and obedience with regard to those who have taken on their shoulders the tremendous burden of government.

Sometimes, those in authority are deserving of our criticism. Do we offer it in a constructive way, without regard for our own interests—with objectivity?

8. If I am in a position of responsibility or authority, do I use this for my own advantage or for the good of others, in a spirit of service?

More often than not, when we hear of a "crisis of obedience," what we are really confronted with is a "crisis of authority." Someone is incompetent in matters of government, and yet holds public office. He or she confuses the noble charge of "governing" with the privilege of "giving orders."

Have I accepted responsibility out of vanity, or out of a desire for "upward mobility," when I knew I would not render efficient service in that responsibility? Have I accepted remuneration for the performance of a service which should have been rendered gratis? Have I taken advantage of my subordinates, abusing their patience by imposing upon them the weight of my authority? Have I obtained my office by virtue of favoritism, or "pork barrel" politics, when others would have been more competent and more deserving? Have I used the things (and persons) placed at my disposition for the more efficient exercise of my office for my own private convenience instead of for the public good? Have I been guilty of vainglory in my office, so that I have an immoderate love of ''making an appearance'' in the media, or at large or prestigious gatherings, merely for my own vain satisfaction?

Have I been guilty of envy or jealousy when someone else has obtained a public charge which I should have liked to have myself? Have I ''bad-mouthed'' anyone because I failed to win this or that position? With regard to my superiors—have I treated them with deference and respect, or have I presented undue obstacles to the implementation of their decisions and dispositions? Have I been negligent in my functions? If my position of authority is that of an independent business person, have I sought to have my employees love me or fear me? Have I treated them as my brothers and sisters, or have I contented myself with looking to the results of their material labor without regard for their well-being in other areas of their lives? Have I been willing to make exceptions to the rules for a just cause in particular cases, or have I been rigid and inflexible in the exercise of my authority?

9. Have I been truthful and fair, or have I injured others by deceit, calumny, detraction, rash judgment, or violation of a secret?

Question 9 covers a broad area, in which we should all examine our consciences in depth. Lying is a real scourge. There are lies that cause great injury, and there are others whose subject and effect do not constitute ''grave matter.'' But in either case, lying degrades human beings, and undermines the relationships of trust and confidence which should exist among them. Some lies are called, ''white lies,'' as if there were nothing wrong with them whatever. But there is no such thing as a lie with which there is nothing wrong whatever. Let our speech be ''yea, yea,'' and ''no, no''—that is, when we say yes, let that mean yes, and when we say no, let that mean no. Let us be ''right out front''—truthful people, who say just what we mean.

As to the second question, let us not forget that it is an obligation in justice to make restitution when we have caused another to lose reputation by our careless tongue—that little organ which, as the Apostle James tells us, can start a conflagration.

Sometimes we hear people say, yes, they did speak ill of someone— but what they said was true. Fine, then this is not calumny, it is simple detraction. If you reveal someone's shortcoming or sin to someone who did not know about it, you are injuring that person's reputation. Rash judgments are always based on suppositions. Now, is a supposition an established fact? Do my judgments not occasion a loss of face on the part of the victims of my statements, and a loss of confidence in them on the part of others?

The way to root out the abominable habit of speaking ill of others is to begin speaking well of them. If he or she has ten vices, and only one virtue, say something about the virtue. This will be the best way to extricate ourselves from the unjust, cruel, loveless position of being "detractors," who seek not "that the sinner be converted and live," but that he or she become mired down in an unhappy situation.

Once more, then: when our detraction has caused someone to suffer a grave loss of reputation, we must restore that reputation. We must make restitution for what we have taken. It will not do to come to confession and say, "I have committed calumny." This is the way to begin, but now I have to restore that lost reputation.

The Ritual asks us whether we can keep a secret, whether we are worthy of receiving confidences. When someone tells *me* something, it is so that *I* will know it—and only I, unless he or she has indicated that it makes no difference who knows it. If that person had wished to make it a public matter, he or she would have chosen a different manner of revealing it. Generally speaking, when someone tells us a "secret," that person has a natural right to expect that no one will come to know it but ourselves.

Have I not been too quick to confide (in confidence, of course!) what has been told me in confidence? There are "secrets" which become public knowledge in a matter of hours! How would I like it if someone told my secrets?

10. Have I done violence to others by damage to life or limb, reputation, honor, or material possessions? Have I involved them in loss? Have I been responsible for advising an abortion or procuring one? Have I kept up hatred for others? Am I estranged from others through quarrels, enmity, insults, anger? Have I been guilty of refusing to testify to the innocence of another because of selfishness?

Every human being is my brother or sister. We have just spoken of possible wounds we may have inflicted on someone's reputation or honor. But people have a right to their physical "integrity," too—their wholeness, their right to life. Have I been violent, using physical force with my fellow human beings? Frequently, or only from time to time? Have I made reparation?

Have I had an abortion? Have I assisted as a doctor or nurse at an abortion? Have I counseled an abortion, or helped procure one for someone else? Have I ever stopped to consider that a human embryo is endowed with *human life*, from the first moment of its conception?

Have I entertained hatred for anyone? If so, has it been a passing hatred, or an enduring one? Does it humiliate me to have to ask pardon of anyone? Have I become fixed in some resentment or other, and refused to take the means to put an end to this abnormal breach in relations, especially with relatives or "in-laws"?

Do I injure my neighbor with insults? If I do, are they deeply and seriously offensive, or are they just "little digs"? When my neighbor is angry, do I try to calm him or her, or do I add fuel to the fire with reasons of my own why he or she *ought* to be angry, when I should be giving reasons for calm and peace? When I have had a "hard day," do I take it out on my family?

Does it sadden me when people are quarreling—or when they are "not speaking"? Or is it "all the same to me"? Have I promptly forgiven those who have offended me, or am I slow to be reconciled with them?

Do I really listen to what another has to say in a discussion or argument, or do I think I am automatically right?

It can sometimes happen that a word from me will set someone in the right who has been falsely accused. If this opportunity has arisen, have I made the attempt to come to another's aid, or have I left this person to his or her fate, so as not to have to "get involved"—or because I had connections with the accusers—or because I thought I had reason to "get even" with the accused—or because I would have suffered a loss of reputation by coming out on the side of "someone of that kind"?

These are all things to think about. Justice, remember, is to be done at all cost. Nothing else should make any difference to me. Besides—how would I wish to have people treat *me* in these situations?

11. Have I stolen the property of others? Have I desired it unjustly and inordinately? Have I damaged it? Have I made restitution of other people's property and made good their loss?

Sometimes we think the Seventh Commandment is only for muggers, or people whose names appear on the police blotter. We are mistaken.

Is it not stealing to overcharge someone? Don't people call it "robbery" when someone puts too high a price on a product? There is something to think about.

If we take something from a store without paying for it, and then come to confession and accuse ourselves of "taking" things, all well and good so far. But we have an obligation to make restitution. We have to give back what we have taken, or its equivalent value. It is true, we need not do so in a way that will ruin our reputation by "giving us away," but there are ways in which restitution can be made without doing so.

An "inordinate desire for other people's property"—who could ever be so terrible to have such a desire? Well, I do, when I concretely, in this or that particular instance, and unjustly, covet the goods of my neighbor. Have I duly resisted this combination of envy and ambition, this "concupiscence of things," this genuinely carnal attitude. Or have I sought instead to "relativize" material goods—to see them in their proper relation to spiritual things, and so to bring order into my appetites?

If I have committed any of these injustices, have I resolved them by restoring the loss I have caused to others? At times it is practically impossible to make restitution to the persons actually stolen from, especially if I have made a habit of stealing from, or overcharging, many different people over a period of time. In this case what I can do is calculate the approximate amount of the total theft and make a donation in that amount to a charitable institution. *Someone* should get the things I have that I should not have.

As we have pointed out, injury and loss inflicted on another are to be repaired. And this applies to physical injury, not just to loss of reputation and so forth. Sacramental confession is a good beginning. But it is not the end—unless I have already made the required restitution before I come to confession.

12. If I have been injured, have I been ready to make peace for the love of Christ and to forgive, or do I harbor hatred and the desire for revenge?

Of course, we are not the only ones to commit injuries and injustices. We also have to suffer offenses committed against us by our brothers and sisters.

One can suffer well or one can suffer badly. Our Lord wants more from us than that we merely "put up with" our brothers and sisters. He wants us to be able to suffer with real patience, and with an attitude that will permit our brother's or sister's conversion. It is not so hard to suffer calumnies, detraction, injustices, insults, and attacks, if I repay them in kind!

When I have been the victim of an injury of some kind, have I committed one in return, so that whereas before there was but one injustice now there are two? Have I been fond of "playing the victim," and gone around looking for sympathy, while making sure everyone knows "who did it"? Or have I kept my secret? Have I sought to accept the evil done me as Christ accepted the evil done him? Have I uttered cries that would pierce the heavens at slight injuries—the kind that are more a matter of human weakness than of malice?

When I have been offended and the other party comes to me seeking my forgiveness, have I been prompt to grant it? Or have I imposed excessive conditions? Have I been one of those people who say, "Sure, I can forgive—but I can't forget!" Some people say they forgive, but deep down in their hearts they harbor a resentment, and make up their minds to have no more dealings with the person who has offended them. Do I live the law of the Gospel and "turn the other cheek"? Or do I follow the old "Lex Talionis," instead, and re-tali-ate with "an eye for an eye and a tooth for a tooth"? Have I plotted revenge, perhaps in complicity with others? If so, have I carried out my purpose, so that now I have injured the other in return, either personally or in his or her family, friends, and so on?

Let us read the question carefully. It does not ask us whether we have been ready to make peace because we are a peaceable type of person, who cannot live for long with a conscience burdened with resentment. This would not be a bad thing, of course. It would show that I have a talent for meekness, that I am a natural peacemaker. But this is not what the question says. No, I am being asked, "Have I been ready to make peace *for the love of Christ?*" This colors the proposition in a new way, of course. The point is to forgive *because our Lord forgave*—to forgive in order to obey his law—as a sign that we love God—as an act of justice, in view of the fact that we would seek to be forgiven ourselves, should the occasion arise.

The desire for revenge is quite "natural." It is one of our primary, primitive instincts. We are creatures of flesh and blood, and it is against "flesh and blood" that we have to war, lest our appetites make animals of us. This instinct, this appetite, blinds. It prevents us from seeing good in others. It will not give us a moment's peace until we have wreaked our vengeance.

It has no place in the following of Christ. It has no place in the project Christ has bequeathed to us of creating a new human being in ourselves and others. Which "appetite" is growing and maturing within me, the appetite for peace or the appetite for revenge? Am I constantly molding a right conscience, a strong conscience, one that will enable me to "suffer well"? Or do I give free rein to the most primitive human instincts?

3. Christ our Lord says: "Be perfect as your Father is perfect."

The law of the Christian says, "Ever onward and upward." It does not consist merely in "not being bad." It consists in being perfect—*because* our Father is perfect and *as* our Father, to whose image and likeness we have been created, is perfect.

Hence we have an obligation to *tend* to this perfection. We shall not always succeed in making great progress. But as long as our good intentions put us on the road, as long as we make a beginning, we shall make progress.

What has the new Ritual to say to us to help us examine our consciences in this respect?

1. Where is my life really leading me? Is the hope of eternal life my inspiration? Have I tried to grow in the life of the Spirit through prayer, reading the word of God and meditating on it, receiving the sacraments, self-denial? Have I been anxious to control my vices, my bad inclinations and passions, e.g., envy, love of food and drink? Have I been proud and boastful, thinking myself better in the sight of God and despising others as less important than myself? Have I imposed my own will on others, without respecting their freedom and rights?

This set of questions opens as if to say, "Let us begin at the begin-

ning. What are my fundamental life options? Where is my life headed?''
If our life is on course right from the beginning, the whole crossing
will be on course too. But if we begin ''a little off,'' then the farther we go
the farther off course we shall be. If God is the fundamental, basic
orientation of my life, then the steps I take to get to him will be the right
ones. I shall choose ''means proportioned to the end.''

But if God is not the end, what is? Social status? More money? The
enjoyment of what the world has to offer? To be ''left in peace,'' not to be
bothered with anyone, not to ''get involved''? Have a family and watch
them grow up and ''get ahead''? But what is ''getting ahead'' for me? Do
I exercise responsible judgment as to my basic orientations? Are my
judgments ''solid rock,'' so that I can structure my life on them?

But for these possible good orientations to become actual in my life, I
have to cultivate them, as one waters a seed so that it may sprout up,
become a tree, and bear fruit. We are challenged to ''grow in the life of
the Spirit,'' the Holy Spirit within us, in imitation of Christ. We are
offered appropriate means of doing so. One of them is prayer.

Do I pray every day? Do I do so as a child or as an adult? Is my prayer
hurried, as if I looked forward to getting it over with? Or do I enjoy it? Do
I ''ask well,'' or do I ask for vanities and foolishness? Am I grateful in my
prayer? Am I a ''worshiper in Spirit and truth''? Am I persevering in
prayer, or do I only pray when things are going badly for me, and slack
off when life starts to go smoothly again?

Do I read the Holy Bible? Do I read it regularly? Do I treat it as a kind
of companion of mine, and keep it where I can look into it attentively and
often? If there are passages which I do not understand, or which cause me
difficulties, do I consult someone about them, so as to extricate myself
from my doubts and solve my difficulties? Do we have family Bible
sessions? If not, do I intend to start them? Do I study the Sunday Readings
ahead of time, so as to go to Mass better prepared? After Mass, do I
sometimes talk over the Readings with my family, or meditate on them
myself? Remember, they are the Word of God.

Do I participate in the sacramental life of the Church, especially in the
Sacraments of Penance and the Eucharist? Do I have the proper disposition? Do I come late for Mass? Do I procrastinate when it comes to going
to confession? Do I realize that the married life is a sacramental life, and

that I ought to be living in the grace that arises from this "great mystery," this great Sacrament?

Have I built a little (or big, for that matter) Catholic library in my home, so that the members of my family may obtain adequate enlightenment and be helped to cultivate their faith?

Do I practice self-denial, so as to try to imitate Christ and thus conquer the passions and inordinate tendencies that habitually estrange me from God and my brothers and sisters? Am I subject to envy—a kind of regret and vexation at the good of another, at the success and well-being of another? Or on the contrary, do I "laugh with him who laughs" and rejoice with people who are happy and doing well? Am I gluttonous? Have I temptations in regard to food and drink? Do I practice the disorder of eating and drinking more than I should, more than my reason tells me is necessary? (Of course, there will be special moments when my table is spread more lavishly, in order to help create a festive atmosphere.)

Our Lord asks me to be meek and humble of heart. He asks me to become as a little child. He asks me to be last if I want to be first. He asks me to be a faithful servant. He asks me to imitate him by not seeking the most important places. But has it not happened on more than one occasion that I have blown myself up like a balloon, and floated up out of where I belonged into a world of false appearances where I could present a façade, a mask, with nothing behind it? Has my pride not prevented me from asking my brother or sister for forgiveness, for fear of losing my reputation or admitting a mistake? Have I not played God just a bit—all-powerful, infallible, vaunting my opinions as if they were certitudes? Have I not sometimes had an "inflated ego," that ignored everything except the great "I"?

Even when performing good works, have I not mixed a bit of vanity with my good intentions, and boasted of what I was doing? Have I belittled the efforts of others, as if my own accomplishments (naturally) were better than theirs? Have I stopped to consider the admirable efforts of my neighbor to overcome his or her difficulties, or do I think I am the only one who struggles to improve?

Very few things are really essential. (Actually, "one thing only" as Jesus told Martha. But let us say, "very few things"). We must always distinguish between these important things and those that are not important—the incidentals, the things that can be this way or that way without changing anything substantial.

Have I not, on occasion, confused what is "substantial," or essential, with what is "accidental," or incidental? Has my self-centeredness, which "draws all things to itself," not made me a dictator with my fellow human beings? Have I done my own will as if it were infallible—as if I were the paragon of virtue and wisdom? Or have I allowed my neighbor to create a little space for himself or herself, where he or she can feel, and be, truly free—a place where my neighbor is secure in the possession and exercise of his or her rights? Have I ever thought about what is meant by the "freedom of the children of God"? Have I shown by my life that I know I have obligations before I have rights?

When you come right down to it, all these things are related to justice. Imposing my will on others, showing them disrespect, prideful attitudes—all these things are actual injuries I do to another. They are real injustices. Never would I wish them for myself. We are very jealous of our liberties. We know that when another's will grows too strong our own begins to weaken. All this we know. But . . . how true it is: "There's many a slip 'twixt the cup and the lip"!

What is being asked of us is that we *take steps* in the direction of being "perfect as our Father is perfect."

2. *What use have I made of time, of health and strength, of the gifts God has given me to be used like the talents in the Gospel? Do I use them to become more perfect every day? Or have I been lazy and too much given to leisure?*

No one can add a single extra minute to his or her life. The Lord knows our length of days, and knows what we are going to do with these hours and minutes that he has entrusted to our stewardship. To waste time is to waste a gift that will *never be given again*. It is letting a moment slip away that will never return. It is an irrecoverable loss.

The opposite of losing something is finding it. When I *find* time, it is mine. I make it mine as the air is mine, when I take it into my body and let it purify me. If I do not waste time, at the end of my days I shall *have* the years I have lived. How many years will many people "have"? Eight hours a day are for repose. Of the sixteen that remain—subtracting the time for my personal needs, for meals, and for the normal "loss of time" in getting from one place to another—how many of these hours do I make my own? And of the hours that I do make my own, how many do I devote to the service of others? (I can only give others what I am myself and what I have myself.) Is it not a fact that many persons are a good deal younger than they say they are? Have I not sadly wasted my life in splendid foolishness?

In all this wasted, squandered time it is only too evident what I have done with my talents. I have hidden them in the earth. I "have not had time" to water them so that they will bear fruit. And God wishes to repay us a hundredfold! What a waste!

We often take account of our sins of *commission*. But we forget that there are sins of *omission*, too. Have I done the good I could have done and should have done? Have I hoarded my talents for my personal enjoyment? Have I been lazy, refusing to "do my best," and thereby robbing society of the talents with which I have been entrusted for the common good? Let us never forget, *all* things are for the glory of God, for my own perfection, and for the perfection of my brothers and sisters—*all* things. What I *do* and what I *have* are useless, if they do not help me to *be* "more and better," and useful to my brothers and sisters.

This is what it means to "make use of the gifts God has given me," in terms of the question the Church is asking us in the examination of conscience we find in the new Rite of Penance. For if these gifts are "given" me, then I must never stop asking myself: For what purpose have I been given these gifts? For whose profit have I received this talent?

3. Have I been patient in accepting the sorrows and disappointments of life? How have I performed mortification so as to "fill up what is wanting to the sufferings of Christ?" Have I kept the precept of fasting and abstinence?

Pain hurts. It is not easy to be patient—to "suffer well." But here too we have Christ as the consummate model for our imitation—Christ, the "Yes" who was contradicted, Christ who had to suffer for his yes. The life of Christ was a continual mortification, a constant struggle to withstand the opposition of those who should have been receiving him with open arms.

Every human being lives a life filled with pain and contradiction, physical and spiritual. Do I bear up under them? Have I gone through my apprenticeship of suffering, and learned to suffer well? Or have I complained about my little aches and pains, forgetting how insignificant they are? Have I sought to call attention to myself when I was ill, exaggerating my discomfort so that people would notice me? Have I lied, and said I was ill when I was not?

Holy Scripture tells us that we are to "fill up what is wanting to the sufferings of Christ." Have I made an effort to understand the redemptive value of pain and illness, or have I viewed them only as something to be rid of, and the sooner the better? Have I shown compassion for those who are ill, in order to help them understand their sufferings and "suffer better"? Have I allowed myself to be overcome by boredom and depression, or have I drawn strength from my weakness, and made an effort to be even more "full of pep" when I did not feel well?

Let us not forget, *everything can and should be incorporated into the salvific plan of Christ. Everything* can be redemptive. *All things* can "work together unto good," unto salvation—mine and my neighbor's. *Everything* has the capacity to be offered up in Christ, to be transformed into sacrifice, into the price of our redemption. Yes, even our pains and afflictions.

The laws of fast and abstinence are only laws of the Church, it is true. There is nothing in the Gospels that directly obliges me to fast on one particular day rather than another. But the fact that neither Christ nor the Apostles have told me I have to fast and abstain on Ash Wednesday and Good Friday, and abstain on all the Fridays of Lent, does not relieve me of my obligation to do so.

On the other hand, it is true that the *spirit* of these penitential acts is more important than the external acts themselves. The main thing is not the "negative act" of not eating. The main thing is *why*. And the reasons why are all summed up in one: the imitation of our Lord Jesus Christ. Thus the Church has now compressed all fasting and abstinence into the framework of Lent. Why? Out of a desire to imitate the suffering Jesus. Out of a desire to draw near to the cross of Christ. It is not a matter of not eating beef and then stuffing oneself with fish or eggs because they are not meat. *It is a matter of denying oneself something.* It is a matter of acquiring a mentality capable of really "relativizing" things. Whether something is meat or not meat is secondary. What is primary is to deprive ourselves of something in order to show that it is possible to deprive ourselves of something. Once we have learned this lesson well, we shall be capable of great privations as well, should the need arise.

This "relativization of goods" will set us on the right road toward an understanding of Christian "eschatology." There are goods that are imperishable. But they are not here, they are not to be found in this present moment. They will appear at the true Banquet of Life, where fast and abstinence will be no more. They will be found in the full, the fulfilled, Kingdom of God. There, there will be no tears, no privations, no need for conversion. Hence there will be no need for penance, either, for all trials, tests, and proofs will have come to an end. There will be no more contests of mettle. This is the moment of the crown, the prize.

Fidelity to the laws of the Church will help us better understand the Gospel. It is true that these laws do not flow directly from the Word of God. But surely the history of so many saints, so many penitents, can instruct us here. They had a sense of the things of God, and (since they were the masters and mistresses of the things of this world) a sense of the things of this world as well. Thus Christ could really be their Lord. It is they who, by their practices, fashioned the customs that have become consecrated today in the laws of the Church concerning self-denial.

4. Have I kept my senses and my whole body pure and chaste as a temple of the Holy Spirit consecrated for resurrection and glory, and as a sign of God's faithful love for men and women, a sign that is seen most perfectly in the sacrament of matrimony? Have I dishonored my body by fornication, impurity, unworthy conversation or thoughts, evil desires, or actions? Have I given in to sensuality? Have I indulged in reading, conversation, shows, and entertainments that offend against Christian and human decency? Have I encouraged others to sin by my own failure to maintain these standards? Have I been faithful to the moral law in my married life?

There is no escaping it, the old catechisms and spiritual writers had a point. They warned us to "guard our senses," to "keep watch over our senses." Not because the senses are evil, of course. Not by any means. Not because the activity of the senses is anything to fear in itself. The reason we are warned to keep watch over our senses is simply that the sense faculties (like the intellectual faculty) can do us a disservice if we do not direct them according to right reason. The Ritual recommends we ask ourselves whether we have kept our senses, and our whole body, "pure and chaste." Now this purity, and this chastity, are not a matter of negative attitudes. They are the reflection of a nature guided harmoniously toward its proper ends, by reason and grace. If my body is nothing but a vessel for the passions, if this is how I define it, then this definition will also define its activities and its purpose. But if, as the Apostle Paul says, my body is the "temple of the Holy Spirit," the place where God dwells and acts, the instrument of his grace—then the question takes on a different tone altogether, and the senses acquire a marvelous vocation; to make manifest not only the human spirit, but God himself who dwells in our hearts.

Have I treated my body as destined to live forever, as the glorified Body of Christ is alive forever? Or have I corrupted my calling, my vocation—and the vocation of a body that has been given me so that the senses can be the receptors and "recognizers" of the invisible world of God? Have I visited prostitutes, purchasing their bodies, and thereby supporting a vile commerce with which we are to have nothing to do? Have I stopped to think that fornication causes the other party to fall from grace as well—when I have the obligation to help that other party along the road to sanctification? Have I ever attempted to help or to convert a prostitute? Have I treated someone as a prostitute who by conventional standards would not be considered such? Have I given myself to a man who is not my husband, oblivious of the fact that Mary, our model, is deep within every woman? Have I sought to excuse my sin and weakness by my "love" for the person to whom I gave myself, saying "I did it for love"?

Have I allowed myself to be carried away by thoughts that sully the dignity of a human being and child of God as if I were watching a pornographic film in my mind, thereby exciting my most primitive passions and most carnal appetites? Am I in the habit of telling impure jokes, and enjoying the jokes of this kind that others tell? Or have I had the moral strength and courage to declare publicly that I dislike this sort of thing?

If anything debases a human being's dignity it is pornography. Pornography is one of the most lucrative commercial enterprises in the West. It is well known that, openly or covertly, pornography makes its way into nearly all countries of the world, especially their large cities. Films, televisions, magazines, and books are the most common vehicles for its distribution. It need not always be refined, or "perfected," as in other, pornographically more "advanced," countries; in Latin America it is generally found in rather coarse and vulgar forms. (But then you've got to start somewhere.) Have I had the delicacy of conscience to select programs and reading calculated to direct my life in the way of transparency and purity? Have I done the same on behalf of my children?

In the area of impurity and sensuality, we have to remember, example spreads like wildfire. Sensuality—or what is called the "mystery of sex," generally meaning we are ignorant of the realities of the matter—provokes curiosity and interest. Our Lord put us on our guard against scandalizing any of his little ones. And so the Ritual asks us in our examination of conscience: "Have I encouraged others to sin by my own failure to maintain" standards of decency and purity? Have I aroused in others a desire to follow me in my vices? Have I attempted to entice them into situations in which their state of grace would be in danger? Have I tempted the innocent? Have I continued to provoke and arouse those who have resisted my invitations in order to make a "conquest"?

Every state of life has laws to govern it. Marriage is no exception. Marriage is a sacramental situation in which spouses share everything in common, including their own bodies. Each belongs to the other.

But there is good belonging and bad belonging. It is not a matter of possession or property. It is not a matter of submission and subordination. It is not a matter of subjugating another, but just the contrary: it is a matter of elevating him or her, of recognizing, and causing him or her to recognize, his or her value and worth as a daughter or son of God. There is a moral law that governs conjugal acts. If this law is not observed, it turns against the spouses. In the Rite of Marriage, the spouses are reminded that Christ blesses their love, and that they are already consecrated in baptism and will now be enriched and strengthened by a special sacrament so that they may assume the duties of marriage in mutual and lasting fidelity, and in the presence of the Church they are asked to state their intentions. The priest then questions them about their freedom of choice, faithfulness to each other, and the acceptance and upbringing of children:

N. and N., have you come here freely and without reservation to give yourselves to each other in marriage? Will you love and honor each other as man and wife for the rest of your lives? Will you accept children lovingly from God, and bring them up according to the law of Christ and his Church?

For those of us who are married, the time has come to ask ourselves: Have we indeed "assumed these responsibilities"? Has our sexual activity as spouses been open to the procreation of life? Have I practiced onanistic or masturbatory acts? Let us not forget, *everything* in our married life is supposed to help the Sacrament of Marriage be a clear sign of Christ's love for his Church by being a love pact between each couple symbolic of God's love-pact with his People.

5. Have I gone against my conscience out of fear or hypocrisy?

There is a principle in moral theology that we must "form our conscience." What does this mean, "form"? It means we must *inform* it. It means we must furnish it with *criteria by which to judge the data* presented to it. Then the judgments it makes according to these criteria will, in turn, cause it to mature, and to "rectify," to grow more and more "right" and "straight."

Very often we make our judgments lightly. We say (and think): "It seems to me . . . I think . . . I guess. . . ." But do we ask ourselves *why* we so "think" or "guess"? On what grounds do I base my affirmations? A "prudential judgment," as it is called, terminates in: "Very well, now do that." But before I arrive at this point in the prudential process, in order to "form my conscience," I must first seek counsel, in order correctly to conceive the means and circumstances which will be required in order for me to perform this or that morally correct act. Secondly, after conceiving the means and circumstances, I must judge the data before me. That is, I must take all the pertinent facts under diligent consideration, in order to conclude what I *should* do, when I should do it, and in what circumstances. Third, and last, I must "order" the counsel I have received, and the judgment I have made of the data, "to action." That is, I must apply the counsel and the judgment in actual practice.

Thus my conscience becomes the "ultimate norm" of my actions. If, *after this threefold process has been completed*, my conscience tells me I should do such and such a thing, then I must do it. But I often hide behind "my conscience" so as to be able to do what *I* want to do. But this is precisely *un*conscientious. Then of course the other possibility is that I *know* what I should do, and how and when and in what circumstances—and I do not do it. This happens very commonly. Now, it is true that my conscience can sometimes have to operate in the presence of violence exerted upon me, or grave fear. But in order to excuse me from culpability, it must be *real* violence, or *grave* fear. When I appeal to violence or fear, then, as my excuse, let me look well whether it has been selfish fear, or hypocritical duplicity, that has moved me to act habitually against my conscience. Is it my reputation I "fear" to lose? Or material things, perhaps?

Have I a weak character, so that I fail to apply an efficacious remedy to these situations, and let my judgment be ruled by that of others? Have we sought to be "on good terms with God and the Devil," switching flags as the occasion suits us? Have I flattered the ears of others, telling them what they like to hear? Or have I always told the truth, "straight out"? Am I a "fence-sitter," refusing to take sides with anyone or anything? Have I confused people as to what my real opinions are, or what I really meant when I said such and so? Let us remember, attitudes like this can be transformed into real tragedy. They can dismantle human beings' most precious institutions by rendering genuine dialogue impossible. Genuine dialogue presupposes sincerity. It presupposes that one acts in accordance with a virtuously rectified conscience. After all, my conscience can be mistaken. I can have corrupted it by withholding information from it, or by supplying it with false data. I can have formed bad habits, which impede the formation of a correct conscience.

6. *Have I always tried to act in the true freedom of the sons of God according to the law of the Spirit, or am I the slave of forces within me?*
More than once we have heard it said (or have said ourselves), "I am a free person. I do what I want." Well, of course, "doing what I want"—physical liberty—is freedom. But it is only rudimentary freedom. To be physically able to do what I want to do is surely not something to be scorned. But it was never the deepest aspect of freedom. The

essence of freedom is not to do what I *want*, but to do what I *should*. And what I *should* do is whatever is good.

Hence the only free person is the one who performs good acts. The person who performs evil acts is the slave of the evil committed. Freedom implies option. Hence no one is more free than the one who opts for, who chooses God and good; and no one is more a slave than the one who rejects God and chooses the ways of evil.

Scripture speaks to us of the "freedom of the children of God." Now, this is not the mere "freedom" of lower creatures, which fulfill their calling by following their instincts in virtue of their nature. Strictly speaking, theirs is not "freedom" at all. They are simply acting in accordance with what nature has determined for a being which is of this kind rather than another. Only the human being has received the vocation and dignity of a son or daughter of God, an "adoptive filiation" in view of the merits of Christ our Brother, who is the only natural Son of God. Christ was the most free of the free. But he was free in obedience. Obedience made him free, even when his hands and feet were nailed to the cross. In like manner, in order to act with the true "freedom" of the children of God, we must "nail" ourselves, in obedience, to the God who bestowed this freedom upon us. The truth that is in this obedience will burst every bond that restrains us. The truth that is in this obedience will enable us to "mortify," kill, little by little, the "old self," the self that is not God's legitimate son or daughter.

The fortunes of the old self are ruled by the law of the flesh. Are we ruled by the law of flesh and blood? Do we live by the laws of the world, fashioned by use, custom, public opinion, and public nonsense? Do we seek to be first in all things, when the law of the Spirit, which would have us imitate Christ, says, "The last shall be first"? Are we "poor in spirit," when the law of the world tells us we have to possess many things, too many things, superfluous and vain things? Am I patient, when the law of the flesh impels me to be the kind of person who "will take nothing from anyone"? Do I know how to "suffer well," investing my suffering and pain with a redemptive value, or—moved by the world of the flesh—have I fled pain as a senseless thing, devoid of any value? Have I hungered and thirsted for justice, desiring the coming of the Kingdom in a world forgetful of all law and right?

Does mercy mean anything to me, or does the world drive me to vengeance, and lead me to turn my eyes away when someone's misery lies in my path? Do I have an upright heart, a heart turned toward the face of God? Or am I immersed in all manner of impurity that sullies the pathways of the Spirit? Do I work for peace, or do I wage a war in my heart, in which flesh cries out against other flesh in a desperate drive to emerge triumphant? When justice is punished, am I the one punished, or is it I who inflict the punishment? Have I ever been accounted a fool for being a Christian—thus suffering the likeness of Christ in my own flesh? Or—so wise to the ways of the world—am I ashamed of the name of Christian?

The Beatitudes offer us a marvelous opportunity to reform our lives according to the law of the Spirit, which gives us to act with the freedom of God's sons and daughters: a law that is the direct opposite of the law of corruption that drives us further and further down into the corrupt condition of old age and death—when what we really need is a rebirth!

Now we have completed our examination of conscience according to the questions proposed to us in Appendix III of the new Rite of Penance (*The Rites of the Catholic Church*, trans. The International Commission on English in the Liturgy [New York: Pueblo Publishing Co., 1976], pp. 441-45). We think that there is a wealth of content in these forms. We have quoted a set of questions, then offered a little commentary. As we have said, these forms of examination of conscience do not exhaust the possibilities for a review of life that a Christian can make. On the contrary, it seems to us that these forms are to be looked upon as guidelines and general notions for a much more particular and personalized examination on the part of each of us. Many of the faithful experience difficulties in the examination of conscience and preparation for a good confession, and the guidelines in the Ritual can be of invaluable assistance in providing the groundwork, the main lines, for coming to know ourselves as Christ knows us. With these broad outlines as a start, we can fill in the details ourselves, and find new points of convergence, genuinely new perspectives in which to view ourselves. Let us let these questions help us to direct our gaze toward Christ, the precious Model of our following and imitation.

C. Examination of Conscience in the Light of the Teaching of the Gospel and the Apostles

In this part of our book we shall offer the reader a compendium of the teaching of Christ as found in the Gospels, and that of the Apostles, who interpret for us what they have received from the Lord, in the rest of the New Testament. We shall have but rare occasion to cite the Old Testament—surely not because we underestimate it, but because the abundance of the material of the New Covenant will be found to be more than sufficient to the end which we have set ourselves: to shed light on the pathways of our life in order to make a good examination of conscience, not according to subjective criteria of our own, but according to the mind of Christ.

It will be seen at a glance that we have not exhausted the possibilities. There is no end to the list of possible cases we could treat. What we have attempted to do is select the most important ones, or the ones which we believe will best further the purpose of our book.

There are many methods we could have selected. We have decided upon an alphabetical list, so that the reader may more easily find the material he or she particularly needs when analyzing his or her personal experience.

The definitions following each title are based on those found in the Dictionary of the Royal Spanish Academy. The biblical passages are taken (as indeed throughout our book) from *The New American Bible* The New Catholic Translation, sponsored by the Bishops' Committee of the Confraternity of Christian Doctrine (New York: Thomas Nelson, Publishers, 1971).

1. Adoration

Adoration is honor and reverence shown to God by the religious worship which is his due. It includes praising him, glorifying him, and serving him.

> At this, Jesus said to him, "Away with you, Satan! Scripture has it:
> 'You shall do homage to the Lord your God; him alone shall you adore."
>
> (Matthew 4:10)

"Yet an hour is coming, and is already here,
when authentic worshipers
will worship the Father in Spirit and truth.
Indeed, it is just such worshipers
the Father seeks.
God is Spirit,
and those who worship him
must worship in Spirit and truth."

(John 4:23-24)

We know we are to adore God alone (Lk 4:8)—as we have also just read in the text from Matthew. If we adore human beings, or things, we have become idolaters, for we have rendered our honor to objects other than God. Have we fallen into this attitude?

Christ was adored by the shepherds (Mt 2:11), by the Magi (Mt 2:11), by the person born blind (Jn 9:38), by his Apostles when he had calmed the storms and just before his ascension (Mt 14:33, 28:17), and by Thomas (Jn 20:28). All these recognized in His Person the God who dwelt in Him. Do we have these attitudes of recognition and admiration of our Lord?

In heaven there will be nothing but adoration and charity. Let us not forget that we are to anticipate this heaven *here and now*.

It does not suffice to be just any sort of adorer of God. We must be adorers "in Spirit and truth." As the Jerusalem Bible says very well apropos of this verse (Jn 4:23): "The Spirit, the principle of rebirth, is also the source and principle of new worship, the source and principle of spiritual worship. This worship is "in truth" because only such a worship responds to the revelation which God makes to us in Jesus."

Is our adoration, our worship, sometimes "in the flesh" instead of "in Spirit"? That is, is it sometimes a search for our own counsel and the satisfaction of our own needs, and an endorsement rather of our condition of creatures than of the God of creatures?

2.   Adultery

Adultery is unlawful carnal union between partners at least one of whom is married.

"You have heard the commandment, 'You shall not commit adultery.' What I say to you is: anyone who looks lustfully at a woman has already committed adultery with her in his thoughts" (Mt 5:27-28).

"The man who marries a divorced woman likewise commits adultery" (Mt 5:32).

He told them, "Whoever divorces his wife and marries another commits adultery against her; and the woman who divorces her husband and marries another commits adultery" (Mk 10:11-12).

"You who forbid adultery, do you commit adultery?" (Rm 2:22).

Scripture shows us that this is a grave sin, even when committed only in desire (Mt 5:27-28), as we have seen in the Word of Christ above. Do we abandon ourselves to these sometimes uncontrolled desires in which we "covet our neighbor's wife" (Gn 20:17)?

By contrast with the conditions the world imposes on us with the teaching of Jesus our Master, do we have a concrete, practical realization of the fact that an attempt to remarry after a sacramental consummated marriage has ended in civil divorce, is adultery, as long as the "former spouse" is still living (Mt 5:32, 19:9; Mk 10:11-12; Lk 16:18)?

None of what we have said excuses us from the charity with which we should treat these cases—keeping in mind, of course, our further duty to help form public conscience aright, especially where youth are concerned, in order to avoid a destructive "indifferentism." Do we show this charity? Do we distinguish between the sin and the sinner?

3. Ambition

Ambition is a burning desire for power, wealth, honor, or fame.

The mother of Zebedee's sons came up to him accompanied by her sons, to do him homage and ask of him a favor. "What is it you want?" he said. She answered, "Promise me that these sons of mine will sit, one at your right hand and the other at your left, in your kingdom." In reply Jesus said, "You do not know what you are asking. Can you drink of the cup I am to drink of?" "We can," they said. He told them: "From the cup I drink of, you shall drink. But sitting at my right hand or my left is not mine to give. That is for those to whom it has been reserved by my Father." The other ten,

on hearing this, became indignant at the two brothers. Jesus then
called them together and said: "You know how those who exercise
authority among the Gentiles lord it over them; their great ones
make their importance felt. It cannot be like that with you. Anyone
among you who aspires to greatness must serve the rest, and
whoever wants to rank first among you must serve the needs of all.
Such is the case with the Son of Man who has come, not to be
served by others, but to serve, to give his own life as a ransom for
the many" (Mt 20:20-28).

From primitive times, human beings have succumbed to the base
passion of inordinate ambition. They have ever sought to build
themselves a "tower with its top in the sky" (Gn 11:4). And we—have
we not sometimes wished to erect a tower of Babel, reaching for the sky
with our own ambitious strength alone, attempting to solve our problems
without the help of God?

How often have we been truly "temerarious"—presumptuous,
foolhardy? How often have we been guilty of a disproportion between our
pretensions and what we were actually capable of (Si 7:4-6)?

Our Lord Jesus Christ is King—King par excellence. Nevertheless he
rejected the offices and honors the world sought to offer him (Jn 6:15).
Do we follow him as the Model for our imitation?

A faith which is mighty in the "power of littleness" will lead us to
imitate the great ones of the Bible. Moses refused an unseemly honor and
preferred to suffer with his people (Heb 11:24). And we? Do we refuse
what is offered us undeservedly? Or on the contrary, do we seek it?

In the Apostolic teaching, the ambitious are ranked among the "enemies of the cross of Christ," for they are "set upon the things of this
world" (Ph 3:18-19). The best "ambition" of the Christian will be to
possess the goods of the Kingdom, in union with Him Who will subject us
sweetly to Himself.

4.   Appearances

Appearances are the external view or aspect of a person or thing. They are
what "appears," not necessarily what *is*.

The two groups came and said to him: "Teacher, we know you are
a truthful man, unconcerned about anyone's opinion. It is evident

you do not act out of human respect but teach God's way of life sincerely'' (Mk 12:14).

Persons and things can be deceiving. They can seem to be something they actually are not. Are we able to judge persons and things aright, or do we deceive ourselves in their regard?

Do we allow ourselves to be carried away by people's appearances, forming unjust judgments of those who do not *seem* to be as we would have them be? Let us not forget what the Gospel tells us: ''Stop judging by appearances and make an honest judgment'' (Jn 7:24).

Do we forget that ''the world as we know it is passing away'' (1 Cor 7:31)? The *real* world exists here only in outline—traced, or sketched, as it were. Its definitive fullness will be found at the end of the ages, when we shall see God face to face. Do we realize this? Or do we ''absolutize'' this present time, instead of ''relativizing'' its appearances?

Christ knew people's interior (Mk 2:8). He could read what was hidden in their hearts (Mt 16:7-8; Lk 5:22, 11:17, 20:23; Jn 6:61). He discerned their devious thoughts and intentions (Mt 9:4, 12:25, 22:15-18). He had no confidence in deceitful appearances (Lk 20:20, Jn 2:23-25, 6:14-15, 25-26). He saw that many of the ''great'' had greedy hearts (Lk 16:14-15). He saw that we are all naked before God (Heb 4:13).

Do we seek to penetrate the heart of others, so as not to attribute any importance to appearances—to this shell that covers them? At the same time, do we drop our own false masks, and show others our true interior?

5.   Authoritarianism

Authoritarianism is a system or manner of exercising power based on unconditional submission to authority. It subjects human beings unduly, and even, in some cases, persecutes or tyrannizes them.

A- dispute arose among them about who should be regarded the greatest. He said: ''Earthly kings lord it over their people. Those who exercise authority over them are called their benefactors. Yet it cannot be that way with you. Let the greater among you be as the junior, the leader as the servant. Who, in fact, is the greater—he who reclines at table or he who serves the meal? Is it not the one who reclines at table? Yet I am in your midst as the one who serves you'' (Lk 22:24-27).

Those who exercise authority—whether in a public or a private capacity, whether in an institution or in a family—ought to know that they are their subordinates' servants: their "juniors." Is this what we do? Do we abuse our authority? Or do we govern with justice (Ep 6:9, Col 4:1), correcting those who have strayed from the right path, offering our help to the weak (1 Th 5:14), and seeking peace and integrity (2 Tm 2:22)?

We ought to obey legitimately constituted authority not merely out of fear, but in conscience, honoring it as given by God (Rm 13:1). Consequently, those in authority may not oppress human beings. They may not debase dignity and make obedience difficult for them.

Do we pray frequently for those in authority, as a duty in justice (1 Tm 2:1-2)? Do we ask God for the conversion of those who abuse their authority? Are we submissive to and respectful of those in authority, as was Christ himself (Mt 17:24-27)?

Jesus condemned authoritarianism on various occasions (Mt 20:25-28; Jn 3:27, 19:11). The whole apostolic teaching does the same, condemning, for example, attempts to obtain unlawful benefits from one's subjects (1 Th 2:9, 2 Th 3:7-10), failure in the just distribution of relief benefits (2 Cor 8:13-15), governing by threats and with partiality (Ep 6:9), and exploiting one's equals (Lk 20:45-47, 1 Cor 6:8, Jm 5:1-6).

Our Lord repeatedly upbraided his disciples for their disputes concerning who was to be the most important in the Kingdom. They understood authority as *power*, as the privilege of lording it over others, and not as a *service of charity and self-dedication* (Mt 18:1, 20:20-28; Mk 9:33-37, 10:35-45; Lk 9:46-48, 22:24-27, 24:21).

Is this not what we often do ourselves—believe that offices or honors somehow make our being greater, when it is only the greatness of our own genuine virtue and goodness, precisely, which will do honor to the office?

The only way to combat our own authoritarianism will be the humble service of our brothers and sisters, beginning with those most in need (Mt 20:25-28, 23:8-11; Mk 9:35; Lk 22:24-27; Jn 13:12-17). The Apostle Paul himself (who had such authority as the father in faith of so many) refrained from abusing it, showing respect for everyone (2 Cor 1:23—2:1, 1 Th 2:3-12). Do we foment division by inordinate and unjust criticism (2 Cor 12:20) so that we undermine legitimate authority?

6.   Avarice

Avarice is the inordinate zeal for the acquisition and possession of riches in order to hoard them.

> Woe to you who join house to house
>   who connect field with field,
> Till no room remains, and you are left to dwell
>   alone in the midst of the land! (Is 5:8)
>   Incline my heart to your decrees and not to gain (Ps 119:36).
>   "Do not lay up for yourselves earthly treasure. Moths and rust corrode; thieves break in and steal. Make it your practice instead to store up heavenly treasure, which neither moths nor rust corrode nor thieves break in and steal" (Mt 6:19-20).
>   "Avoid greed in all its forms. A man may be wealthy, but his possessions do not guarantee him life" (Lk 12:15).
>   Do not deceive yourselves: no . . . thieves, misers . . . will inherit God's kingdom (1 Cor 6:9-10).

Jesus condemns covetousness and greed, or avarice (Mk 7:22). Have we ever asked ourselves why? After all, what harm can it do?

And he repeats his teaching (Lk 12:15), contrasting the goods of the present, and their insecurity, with those that are to be sought and taken "by force": those of the Kingdom (Mt 11:12).

Anyone, rich or poor, can be greedy. Of course, it is a greater danger for the rich. But the Apostle puts us on our guard: we are not to "rely on so uncertain a thing as wealth," but are to place our hope in "that life which is life indeed" (1 Tm 6:17, 19). Are we excessively attached to things? Do we seek superfluities as if they were necessities? Do we not know that what is superfluous cannot be ours, but must be offered to those who lack necessities?

Let us fear the consequences of avarice. Let us consider why and for whom we accumulate things (Lk 12:13-21).

7.   Blasphemy

Blasphemy is the utterance of words that are insulting to God, the Blessed Virgin Mary, or the Saints.

> "Wicked designs come from the deep recesses of the heart . . .
> blasphemy . . . (Mk 7:21-22).
>   "That, I assure you, is why every sin, every blasphemy, will be
> forgiven men, but blasphemy against the Spirit will not be for-
> given" (Mt 12:31).

Blasphemy in the strict sense of the word is only what is given in the
definition above.

Christ was accused of blasphemy because he proclaimed himself to
be the Son of God (Mt 26:65).

Blasphemy is not a sin that is very frequently committed "formally."
But it certainly is often committed "materially." That is, the blasphem-
ous words we utter are not often *meant* blasphemously, but the fact
remains that words *are* used blasphemously.

Do we casually pronounce words or expressions that are injurious to
God, our Lord Jesus Christ, Mary, or the Saints? Do we not realize, when
we pronounce them in a moment of annoyance, that we are referring to
the noblest objects of our respect and veneration?

Let us not fall into "blasphemy against the Spirit"—which consists
in such a fixation in evil that we are blinded to the salvific deeds of the
Holy Spirit.

Blasphemy is against the Second Commandment, which forbids us to
take the name of God in vain.

8.   Christian Duties

Christian duties are the things to which a Christian is obliged by
ecclesiastical precept, or by other laws natural or positive.

> I declare and solemnly attest in the Lord that you must no longer
> live as the pagans do—their minds empty, their understanding
> darkened. They are estranged from a life in God because of their
> ignorance and their resistance; without remorse they have
> abandoned themselves to lust and the indulgence of every sort of
> lewd conduct. That is not what you learned when you learned
> Christ! I am supposing, of course, that he has been preached and
> taught to you in accord with the truth that is in Jesus: namely, that
> you must lay aside your former way of life and the old self which
> deteriorates through illusion and desire, and acquire a fresh,

spiritual way of thinking. You must put on that new man created in God's image, whose justice and holiness are born of truth (Ep 4:17-24).

St. John imposes on us, as our great obligation, *to be children of the light* (1 Jn 1:5-7). Are we? Do we love the darkness and its works more than we love the day? Do we put the commandments in practice, especially that of "fraternal charity," the love of our brothers and sisters (1 Jn 2:3-11, 3:11-15)?

We have a positive duty to *confess our sins and do penance* for them (1 Jn 1:8-9, 2:1-2), and to keep the commandments (1 Jn 2:3-6), regarding them as the law of life. Do we do this? Do we confess frequently, and with efficacious repentance and sorrow of heart?

We have a negative duty *not to love the world* (in St. John's sense of "world," that is, whatever is contrary to Christ—1 Jn 2:15-17), and to be on our guard against whatever can separate us from the true teaching of Jesus (1 Jn 2:18-24). Are we attached to the "flesh," in such a way that we waft to and fro in the winds of current opinion?

We are the sons and daughters of God, and it is our Christian duty to behave as such. Accordingly we have the obligation of living according to the dignity of this adoption (1 Jn 2:29, 3:1-2), for our hallmark is holiness (1 Jn 3:3-7), while the mark of the "children of evil" is sin (1 Jn 3:8-10).

We are all children of the same Father. Hence *we are one another's brothers and sisters*, and we have obligations pertaining to this condition. If we fulfill these obligations, we shall be wearing the badge of charity, and the world will know that Christ and his promises have not been in vain (1 Jn 3:11-15). After all, love is expressed in the *deeds* of love (1 Jn 3:16-18).

What is our definition of "sons and daughters" of God, or of "brothers and sisters" of one another? When we hear the words of the Apostle John (1 Jn 4:1-6), do we act accordingly? Do we take Holy Scripture seriously? Do we try to penetrate its meaning with all our heart?

The first great duty of a Christian is to *love God and our brother and sister*, for God has loved us first (1 Jn 4:7-11; 1 P 1:22-25, 2:1). If we do so, God will abide deep within us, and all our fear will vanish (1 Jn

4:12-19). We can begin to act in this way by believing in Jesus as God's Anointed Son, the Messiah, and by believing that heaven gives testimony to him (1 Jn 5:5-12).

We have a general Christian duty to *lead a life worthy of our calling*, by the practice of the virtues and in the communion of peace (Ep 4:1-6). For we are called to be saints (1 P 1:13-15, 22-25). Do we conscientiously practice the virtues in concrete cases, so as to fulfill our duties as Christians (2 P 1:3-15)?

Negatively, we have the duty to *flee all evil*. This is not cowardice, but intelligent prudence (Ep 4:25-31, 5:3-14). We are to exercise vigilance, fortitude, prudence, temperance, and trust in God (1 P 5:5-11, Ep 5:15-18). We are members of a living Body, the Body of Christ, and we must be living, active members—we must *struggle*, and fight the good fight (Ep 6:10-20).

We have the Christian duty to *mortify our passions* (Col 3:5-9), stripping off the old self and putting on Christ (Col 3:9-11). Are our attitudes those of Adam, or those of the New Adam, Christ? Do we ask ourselves how Jesus would have discharged the obligations we find ourselves under? How would he have shown his sense of responsibility? How would he have shown solidarity with others and commitment to their needs, how would he have behaved when confronted with doubt. How would he have given testimony to his convictions, even when persecuted for them? How would he have handled our temptations had it been he in our place?

We have the Christian duty to *become involved with our brothers and sisters and their society* (Mt 24:45-51). Our faith in no way diminishes the *responsibility* with which we are to live in the world (Mt 7:24-27)—which must be carried to the point of total self-sacrifice if necessary (Mt 10:24-25; Lk 22:17).

9. Compassion

Compassion is a sense of tender pity for the toil, misfortune, or unhappiness of another.

> At the sight of the crowds, his heart was moved with pity. They were lying prostrate from exhaustion, like sheep without a shepherd (Mt 9:36). Jesus called his disciples to him and said: "My

heart is moved with pity for the crowd. By now they have been with me three days, and have nothing to eat. I do not wish to send them away hungry, for fear they may collapse on the way" (Mt 15:32-33). The Lord was moved with pity upon seeing her [the widow of Naim] and said to her. "Do not cry" (Lk 7:13). Jesus said, "Father, forgive them; they do not know what they are doing" (Lk 23:34).

Compassion is not a mere sentiment. If it were, it could be adequately expressed in a sympathetic word. But *com-passion* means to "suffer with" someone. Hence it must be a matter of *deeds*. Compassion actually lightens the burden of our brother or sister who has fallen into misfortune, because the compassionate person actually helps him or her to carry it (Gal 6:2).

Compassion is an attitude of goodness, pity, and mercy, which does away with hardness of heart, and impels us to solidarity with the misery of others. Are we concerned about, do we show compassion for, our brothers and sisters in material need? Do we participate in any enterprise for the common good which brings compassion to others' suffering? And what of the spiritual needs revealed to us in this world, where so many of our brothers and sisters suffer misery? Do we make any effort to offer them a remedy, and compassionate counsel, as Christ did with the widow of Naim, the family of Lazarus, the leper, the person born blind from birth, and so many others?

Are we hard-hearted and insensitive toward others' suffering and pain (Mt 23:13-33; Mk 3:5, 12:40, 8:1-11).

Let us not forget that only the compassionate become neighbors to a stranger, as did the Good Samaritan (Lk 10:30-37)—and as in the tender story of the father abandoned by his prodigal son (Lk 15:25-32). The Good Samaritan, and the good father, had "bowels of compassion," and they applied real, efficacious remedies to the suffering of unfortunate persons.

What does our own compassion look like? If we could see our heart in a mirror, would it look like a heart of flesh or a heart of stone?

10. Contentiousness

Contentiousness is disputatiousness, a spirit of recrimination, or over-argumentativeness when confronted with the opinions of others.

In everything you do, act without grumbling or arguing (Ph 2:14). Keep reminding people of these things and charge them before God to stop disputing about mere words. This does no good and can be the ruin of those who listen (2 Tm 2:14). For as long as there are jealousy and quarrels among you, are you not of the flesh? And is not your behavior that of ordinary men? (1 Cor 3:3). I fear that when I come I may not find you to my liking, nor may you find me to yours. I fear I may find discord . . . outbursts of anger . . . (2 Cor 12:20). Let us live honorably as in daylight; not in carousing and drunkenness, not in sexual excess and lust, not in quarreling and jealousy (Rm 13:13). "Blest are you when they insult you . . . and utter every kind of slander against you because of me" (Mt 5:11).

When we speak of contentiousness, we do not mean simple "argumentativeness," as may sometimes appear in any earnest, but rational, discussion. We mean an irrational, capricious disputatiousness, charged with animosity and a desire to gain the upper hand. Insults and affronts come easy in an "argument" characterized by this spirit, and these generate new contention, ever deepening discord, and the destruction of peace.

The roots of our contentiousness are those wellsprings of discord, the unmortified passions (Jm 4:1-10).

James lists the things that make us violent people. Our Lord asks us instead to be "meek" in the face of evils (Mt 5:38-42). Rarely do we see Christ exercise violence—and when he does so, his sole interest is the glory of God (Mt 21:12-13; Jn 2:15). There is no place for violence in the salvific plan of God (Mt 26:51-56; Lk 9:54-56; Rm 12:14, 18; 2 Cor 13:11; Heb 12:14). The only "violence" we may be allowed to use is the "violence" of those who snatch God's Kingdom from Him (Mt 11:12)!

Are we meek, or are we violent?

Jesus likewise puts us on our guard against idle words and insults (Mt 5:22-24). Let us remember, just as good words and deeds inspire people to good words and deeds of their own, so one harsh word calls forth another, even harsher one. The Word of God's revelation exhorts us to be strangers to all manner of irate word (Ep 4:31).

11. Correction

Correction—what the old spiritual writers called *correptio fraterna*,

"fraternal correction"—is any action taken to assist someone to correct his or her sins, shortcomings, or defects, including reprehension or censure of these defects.
"If your brother should commit some wrong against you, go and point out his fault, but keep it between the two of you. If he listens to you, you have won your brother over. If he does not listen, summon another, so that every case may stand on the word of two or three witnesses. If he ignores them, refer it to the church. If he ignores even the church, then treat him as you would a Gentile or a tax collector" (Mt 18:15-17). But since it is the Lord who judges us, he chastens us to keep us from being condemned with the rest of the world (1 Cor 11:32). The ones who do commit sin, however, are to be publicly reprimanded, so that the rest may fear to offend (1 Tm 5:20). We exhort you to admonish the unruly . . . be patient toward all (1 Th 5:14). The discipline of the Lord, my son, disdain not; spurn not his reproof. For whom the Lord loves he reproves, and he chastises the son he favors (Pr 3:11-12; cf. Heb 12:5-6).

To love people means to wish them well—will their good. Consequently, to correct someone's vice or defect is to love him or her.

Christ gives us an example of "fraternal correction" when he corrects his disciples for their desires for revenge (Mt 18:22; Lk 9:55-56), their ambition (Mt 20:22-28), their pride (Mt 16:22-23), and their presumption (Lk 22:23-24; Jn 21:15-17). He also upbraids them for their "little faith" (Jn 20:29), and for their purely human outlook on history (Mt 16:22-23).

Is Jesus not also correcting and upbraiding us? Do we not feel ourselves to be included in the cases he corrects?

But correction has its laws, and we have read them in the first of our passages above, the one from Matthew. Christian correction is not "getting even." It is converting the other (Mt 18:15-17), bringing him or her back to full communion with the Church

Do we not often fail in this *right and duty* of charity, out of cowardice, human respect, or the belief that the other party will refuse to accept our correction? But is it not the worst "solution" of all to "leave things the way they are"—that is, leave me with my silence and my brother or sister with his or her sin?

12. Cowardice

Cowardice is a lack of spirit and courage.

Jesus was sleeping soundly, so they made their way toward him and woke him: "Lord, save us! We are lost!" He said to them: "Where is your courage? How little faith you have!" Then he stood up and took the winds and the sea to task. Complete calm ensued . . . (Mt 8:25-26). "There will be signs in the sun, the moon, and the stars. On the earth, nations will be in anguish. . . . Men will die of fright in anticipation of what is coming upon the earth" (Lk 21:25-26). Finally . . . they sighted Jesus approaching the boat, walking on the water. They were frightened, but he told them, "It is I; do not be afraid" (Jn 6:19-20). "Do not be distressed or fearful" (Jn 14:27).

Cowardice and fearfulness are properties of weak, fallen humanity. Further, these properties feed on the indigence and extreme need in which the evil of sin has left us.

Nevertheless, in Jesus' apparitions to his disciples after the Resurrection he repeatedly told them, "Fear not." His presence calms the soul, and our weakness disappears when he is with us.

Have we been courageous in proclaiming the truth about the God who delivers us, sets us free? Have I proclaimed him without fear of reprisal, and without human respect (Mt 5:16, 10:17-21, 24:14; Lk 12:2-4). God does not wish us to be temerarious, or foolishly daring. But he does wish us to be courageous, with a "holy daring"—relying not on our own strength, but on the might of Him who is at work within our littleness (Ep 1:19, 3:16, 6:10-20).

Jesus shows himself to us as the Courageous One, in the trials he has to suffer before he mounts the cross (Mt 27:11-23; Lk 23:8-12; Jn 18:13—19:14). He demonstrates serenity and fearlessness before the scholars of the Law and Herod (Lk 13:31-33; Jn 11:7-10), and praises these qualities in John the Baptist (Mt 11:7-9, 3:7-12, 4:12, 14:3-12).

One of the worst, most pernicious attitudes we can have is cowardice, out of human respect, or for fear of "what people will say," or as manifested in an indefinite procrastination of our duty of frankness in the vain hope that "things will take care of themselves." Is this a description of ourselves?

13. Death

Death is the cessation of life, and occurs when the soul leaves the body.

> Indeed, we know that when the earthly tent in which we dwell is destroyed we have a dwelling provided for us by God, a dwelling in the heavens, not made by hands but to last forever. We groan while we are here, even as we yearn to have our heavenly habitation envelop us. This it will, provided we are found clothed and not naked. . . . The lives of all of us are to be revealed before the tribunal of Christ so that each one may receive his recompense, good or bad, according to his life in the body (2 Cor 5:1-3, 10). If we have been united with him through likeness to his death, so shall we be through a like resurrection (Rm 6:5). But as it is, Christ is now raised from the dead, the first fruits of those who have fallen asleep. Death came through a man; hence the resurrection of the dead comes through a man also (1 Cor 15:20-21).

Have we faith in "life everlasting"? Or is death for us the end of everything?

Do we cooperate with Christ our Life, by whom redemption came into the world, in the definitive conquest of death (Rm 5:17-19)?

Do we realize that sin is death (Rm 6:23), and that, by contrast, the fruit of good works is life (Gal 6:9-10)?

One day's fidelity will not do. In order to conquer death and receive the crown of life, it is necessary to persevere daily, and persevere to the end (Rv 2:10), for we know neither the day nor the hour when the Lord will summon us before his tribunal (Rv 3:3).

The fact that we so dislike the prospect of death, and are so saddened by it, is a sign that we are not born to die, but to live. Death, together with sin, is the greatest scandal of all. Do we often reflect on the close relationship between *sin and death* (Rm 5:12-21, 23; 1 Cor 15:21)? Do we realize that the author of death is the Devil—as he is also the author of the numerous little "deaths" that afflict us (2 Cor 2:11; Ep 2:2; 1 P 5:8-9; 1 Jn 25:19).

We shall be judged according to our works of life and our works of death. *Now is the hour* of the drama of our birth to life or our birth to death. Christ, our Just Judge, will mete out reward and punishment (1 Cor 5:10; Rm 2:6-7).

When we hear of *heaven and hell*, do we consider these realities to be children's stories, far removed from any concerns of our own? Or do we recognize the reality and importance of resurrection to life (Mt 18:10; 1 Cor 13:1), or resurrection to death and the loss of love forever (Mt 25:41; 2 Th 1:8-9; Rv 21:8)?

The battle of Life and Death is already being fought, in our own lives today. Our physical death will be the end of our time of merit (Jn 9:4). How do we react to the death of our dear ones? With hope? Or with desperation? Do we rebel against God and his goodness, saying, "He could have prevented this"? It is normal to feel sorrow when our loved ones are torn away from us, but do we also think about the joy of the good things of the life to come, as our faith and our hope teach us (1 Cor 2:9; 1 Jn 3:2)?

Do we perform the duty we have in justice and mercy to help the members of our family "die well," procuring them the assistance of a priest and the consolation of the sacraments? Do we pray for the departed, and have Masses offered for them? Do we consider them "dead"—or do we consider them as they really are: "living with Christ?"

We know that Christ has vanquished death, his last enemy (1 Cor 15:26). With St. Paul we can now cry: "O death, where is your victory? O death, where is your sting?" (1 Cor 15:55).

We ought to consider *abortion* one of the great signs of sin and death. It is a despicable murder, unjustifiable in every respect, committed against a defenseless, innocent human being. When the mother cooperates in it, it is a perversion of the very meaning of motherhood.

Have we considered that life is sacred from the first moment of conception? Have we performed, or cooperated in, an abortion, whether directly or by recommending it? Do we seek to form clear notions about abortion in our children, showing them why a directly intended abortion is wholly evil, even to save the life of the mother, or even to prevent the birth of a deformed, handicapped, or retarded child?

14. Envy

Envy is sadness or regret at the good fortune of another.

Where there are jealousy and strife, there are also inconstancy and all kinds of vile behavior (Jm 3:16). Where do the conflicts and disputes among you originate? Is it not your inner cravings that make war within your members? What you desire you do not obtain, and so you resort to murder. You envy and cannot acquire, so you quarrel and fight (Jm 4:1-2). When the Jews saw the crowds they became very jealous and countered with violent abuse whatever Paul said (Ac 13:45). So strip away everything vicious . . . jealousies, and disparaging remarks of any kind (1 P 2:1).

Just as one who loves rejoices at the good fortune of the loved one, so envy, this "sorrowful form of hatred," is sad and afflicted at the triumph and success of the neighbor. Love is never envious (1 Cor 13:4).

The sentiment of sorrow at another's good fortune is nearly always accompanied by the desire that it cease to be his or her good fortune and become mine instead. Am I envious? If I am, do I make an effort to overcome this perversion of nature?

Experience shows that envy is bound up with grumbling, complaining and backbiting. In order to wrest good fortune out of the hands of another, I generally have to deprive that other of his or her good repute in people's minds, and thereby rob him or her not only of the good I wish to acquire for myself, but of his or her greatest possession as well: a good reputation.

Do we fall into this miserable vice, which, before it manages to rob the other of his or her good fortune, robs ourselves of joy in what we already have? Do we make a reasonable effort to be content with what we have, with what we need, in order not to have to envy others? Does envy not frequently go hand in hand with an inordinate, insatiable, all-devouring appetite to possess everything we possibly can? Do we realize that envy is a cause of disorder and evil works in our lives, especially of cupidity and greed (Jm 3:16)?

15.　Failure

Failure is the untoward, undesirable, and unexpected outcome of any project.

"Teacher," a man in the crowd replied, "I have brought my son to you because he is possessed by a mute spirit. Whenever it seizes him it throws him down. . . . Just now I asked your disciples to expel him, but they were unable to do so" (Mk 9:17-18). Then Paul stood up in the Areopagus and delivered this address: "Men of Athens, I note that in every respect you are scrupulously religious. . . . God may well have overlooked bygone periods when men did not know him; but now he calls on all men everywhere to reform their lives. He has set the day on which he is going to 'judge the world with justice' through a man he has appointed— one whom he has endorsed in the sight of all by raising him from the dead." When they heard about the raising of the dead, some sneered, while others said, "We must hear you on this topic some other time." At that point, Paul left them (Ac 17:22, 30-33).

We must be neither excessively enthusiastic in success nor depressed in failure.

Failures are but the manifestation of our weakness. Often they are God's warning to us not to be puffed up with pride, and his invitation to perseverance and fortitude.

Persecution and death were the "failures" Jesus' disciples had to undergo as a test of their fidelity (Mt 5:10-12, 10:17-21; Jn 15:18—16:4). Our failures, as well, ought to be considered as moments of trial, lest we place our trust in our poor strength instead of in the power of God.

Christ's failures scandalized his disciples (Mt 16:21-23, 17:22-23; Mk 8:31; Lk 24:17-27). Are we likewise not tempted in various ways in the face of failures of our own (Mk 14:32-42)? Do we accept our successes with humility? Do we accept our failures with fortitude, or do we try to "find out who is to blame" for our own inadequacies? Are we invaded by dejection when we fail to triumph?

16. Faith

Faith is the first of the three theological virtues. It is a supernatural light and knowledge by which, without seeing, we nevertheless believe what God says and the Church proposes to us, on the authority of God himself, which he reveals to us and by which he reveals his plan.

Faith is confident assurance concerning what we hope for, and conviction about things we do not see (Heb 11:1). His commandment is this: we are to believe in the name of his Son, Jesus Christ, and are to love one another as he commanded us (1 Jn 3:23). Faith in the heart leads to justification, confession on the lips to salvation (Rm 10:10). "Whoever acknowledges me before men, I will acknowledge before my Father in heaven" (Mt 10:32).

Holy Scripture frequently uses "faith" as a synonym for trust, piety, certainty, authenticity, and constancy, besides using it in its proper sense.

Without faith it is impossible to love God—this God who exists and who rewards those who seek him (Heb 11:6). Accordingly, faith is a cause of salvation (Mt 9:22; Mk 5:34; Lk 7:50, 8:48, 50, 17:19). Do we seek God with a sincere heart? Do we seek him where he is—in the Church?

Christ does not ask us to have an irrational faith. Quite the contrary, he demands that we believe in him on the basis of the signs he has worked (Mt 9:1-8; Jn 10:25, 37-38, 11:41-44), and he leads us to deepen our faith in humility and confidence (Mt 15:21-28). Do we have the wrong kind of "blind faith," and believe "just because"—without attempting to understand any of the reasons for believing?

Faith goes beyond the conclusions to which we can come by our own strength (Mk 4:37-41), and demands a renunciation of the prejudices of merely human wisdom (Jn 3:3-12). Do we believe in a God we cannot see, or do we demand to feel him with our hands, so to speak, like the Apostle Thomas, who thought he needed to see in order to believe (Jn 20:25)?

Christ insists that we must have faith in order to attain to the salvation offered by his Father (Mt 8:10-13, 9:22, 28-29, 15:21-28; Lk 8:21, 11:28; Jn 1:6-18, 8:24, 30-59)—but not a faith that would be a mere intellectual assent, rather, one that will express itself in works of charity (Jn 15:1-17; Mt 7:17-27, 21:28-32; Rm 2:6; Jm 2:14-16). Indeed, faith is living the life of Christ himself, and joining ourselves to him (Jn 17:1-26; 2 Cor 5:14-21, 13:4-5; Gal 3:26-28; Col 3:3-17).

Is this a description of our faith? Are we able to identify with Christ in his person, his words, and his works?

In antiquity, idolatry was considered to be *the* great sin (1 Cor 6:9-14; 1 Jn 5:21). Is it not still the great sin today? Do we not fashion ourselves "paper gods" and idols to replace the true God? Our "I," our reputation, our status, our money, our titles, our culture, our power, our influence— do these not make God unnecessary for us? Do we put our faith in these "things of the flesh"?

Are we superstitious? If so, it is nothing new (Ac 8:9). Do we try to replace God with a horoscope in the newspaper? Do we seriously believe in fortune-telling, or clairvoyants, or miraculous cures that have nothing to do with our faith in God? Do we trust this "lucky" thing or that one to extricate ourselves from the countless perplexities and "troubles" of our daily life? Especially, do we rely on "preternatural" influences to "solve things"? Our Lord and the Church, offer us simpler, more effective remedies—and more intelligent ones. Do we run after any and every rumored new "apparition" we may hear of, such as of the Blessed Virgin Mary?

Have we been "un-faithful," after having heard and learned the Word of God (Jn 15:22; Rm 1:20-21, 2:6-8)?

Have we allowed ourselves to be carried away by *false or heretical teachings*, ignoring the magisterium of the Church (2 P 2:10, 15, 17; Gal 1:7-9; 2 Tm 3:1-2, 8)? Are we attracted by the latest novelty, attributing more importance to the opinion or pundit we happen to like best, instead of to the teachers of our true faith (2 P 3:3-4)?

Are we the victims of *religious ignorance*, tossed about by the winds of opinion, and lacking a firm foundation in solid doctrine (1 Cor 15:34; Rm 1:25)? Do we put our knowledge of the faith to charitable use by placing it at the disposition of our brothers and sisters (1 Cor 8:11; 1 Tm 6:20-21; 2 Tm 4:3-4; Tt 3:9)?

Faith without love is a dead faith, this is true. But faith is nonetheless important. Do we consider it a matter of great importance to foster our own formation in faith, by reading the Word of God, by building a Christian library in our homes, by subscribing to the diocesan paper, and by reading the discourses of the Pope as they appear, as well as the other instruments of the magisterium of the Church?

If not—shall we begin? Let us not forget, one cannot love a God one does not know. What do we know of God? What God do we know? Could we give a five minute explanation to a pagan of who Jesus Christ is, and of our objective motives for believing in him?

17. Family

A family is a group of related persons who live under the authority of one or more of their number.

"Isn't this the carpenter's son? Isn't Mary known to be his mother and James, Joseph, Simon, and Judas his brothers? Aren't his sisters our neighbors? Where did he get all this?" (Mt 13:55-56). He went down with them then, and came to Nazareth, and was obedient to them. His mother meanwhile kept all these things in memory (Lk 2:51).

Christ is presented in the Gospels as the member of a family (Mt 12:46-47; Mk 3:31-32; Jn 2:12). He had "brothers and sisters," as cousins and other near relatives were called in those days.

No one can have any doubt as to Christ's love for families. He elevates the status of marriage (Mt 19:3-12; 1 Cor 7:1-11, 25-28; Ep 5:22-33), takes part in the joyful celebration of a wedding (Jn 2:1-12), and has intimate friends and visits them at home (Mt 9:10; Lk 7:36, 19:5; Jn 11:1-54; Mk 7:24).

Christian marriage is an institution of Christ (Ep 5:31-32), in which the spouses love each other as Christ and the Church love each other (Ep 5:25-26). Do I love my wife as Christ loves the Church? Do I respect her? Do I reverence her as the head of my household? Or on the contrary, do I demean her, and make use of her as if she were an object (1 Cor 7:3-5, 33-34; Ep 5:25-33; Tt 2:4; Col 3:19)?

The great properties of the state of matrimony are community of love and life, offspring, and the sacramentality that elevates human love to the level of the divine. Have I promoted this state, or neglected it?

Jesus himself declared the monogamy (Mt 19:4-5; Mk 10:6-8; 1 Cor 7:2) and indissolubility of marriage (Mk 10:11-12; Mt 19:9; Lk 16:18; Rm 7:2-3; 1 Cor 7:10-11, 39). His judgment concerning divorce is strict and clear. Do we sometimes criticize the Church for being "too strict" about divorce—for "not caring about the happiness" of the spouses, because it forbids them to "start a new life"—forbids them to divorce one another and remarry?

Where *family planning* is concerned, the Church asks married couples to exercise "responsible parenthood"—accordingly, to refrain from the use of morally reprehensible methods to attain a desired end. Have we thought about the lack of respect for human nature implied in the use of contraceptives, such as condoms, "the Pill," the IUD (which causes abortion), and so on? Or have we attempted to prevent conception by withdrawal? Even from a purely medical point of view, these methods can be unhealthy. For instance, the last named is a frequent cause of frigidity in the female.

Do my spouse and I occasionally reflect on the fact that the virtue of temperance is required in marriage too if no more children are desired?

Faithful to the following of Christ, the Church teaches us that the only acceptable method of birth control is conjugal continence with the rhythm (Ogino-Knaus) method or the observation of one's basal temperature or vaginal secretions (Billings method).

Is the Holy Family our model in our marital and family relationships, as it should be?

What should be the behavior of a *son or daughter* of a family? He or she should be obedient, as Christ was obedient to his Father (Heb 5:8; 2 Tm 3:2; 1 P 2:14; Col 3:20; Ep 6:1), should not spurn parental correction (Heb 12:5, 7), should allow himself or herself to be guided by the Spirit (Rm 8:14), and should live a life of *true* liberty (Rm 8:21), living by faith in Jesus (Gal 3:26; Tt 1:6), imitating God (Ep 5:1), and walking in the way of truth (3 Jn 4; 2 Jn 4).

Are we good children of God and our parents? Do we look down on them for being "old," or "old-fashioned"? Do we lie to them? Do we sadden them by failing to faithfully fulfill our scholastic duties, or the other duties of our state of life? Do we take their money without their knowledge?

How should a *father and mother* behave? They should not be "too hard on" their children (Ep 6:4): they should not push their capacity for patience and obedience to the limit. They should provide for their legitimate needs (2 Cor 2:14), love them with all their heart (Lk 1:17), correct them with justice and equity (Heb 12:7), teach them to worship God and venerate the Blessed Virgin and the Saints, teach them to pray (especially by example), guide them in the correct use of money (without miserliness, and yet with restraint), and refrain from scandalizing them by bad example or discord.

Do we do all these things? Are we negligent in our care of our children? Do we over-protect them? Do we engage in real dialogue with them?

The bonds of flesh and blood are mighty, and they are good. But our Lord wants us to go further. My real "relatives" are those who do the will of God, those who seek to be saints (Lk 2:48, 14:26; Jn 6:40; Mt 12:46-50). Do we value the spiritual bonds that unite Christians among one another? Do we treat all the baptized as our "relatives," our family?

The law of universal Christian love transcends ties of flesh and blood. And so, will it not be eminently in keeping with justice and charity if childless couples, living in a happy marriage *adopt a child*? Will this not be an admirable act of reparation in love, for the un-love that has brought about the situation of this child deprived of parents? Most children available for adoption, remember, are not orphans, but abandoned. Now an abandoned innocent will be surrounded with love. Now an unwanted child will find himself or herself very much wanted. An infant with a most uncertain and difficult future will now find the security and normal life of hearth and home.

And *siblings*? How do we behave with one another? Do we live in union and concord? Or do we vex our parents with our useless squabbling?

18. Forgiveness

Forgiveness is pardon: the remission of due punishment, or the pardon of an offense undergone, or the pardon of or any pending debt or obligation.

> There the people at once brought to him a paralyzed man lying on a mat. When Jesus saw their faith he said to the paralytic, "Have courage, son, your sins are forgiven" (Mt 9:2). "When you stand to pray, forgive anyone against whom you have a grievance so that your heavenly Father may in turn forgive you your faults (Mk 11:25—Compare, "Forgive us our sins for we too forgive all who do us wrong: and subject us not to the trial"—the "Lord's prayer," Lk 11:4). If anyone has given offense he has hurt not only

me, but in some measure, to say no more, every one of you. The punishment already inflicted by the majority on such a one is enough; you should now relent and support him, so that he may not be crushed by too great a weight of sorrow. I therefore beg you to reaffirm your love for him (1 Cor 2:5-8). "Be on your guard. If your brother does wrong, correct him; if he repents, forgive him" (Lk 17:3-4). "I tell you, that is why her many sins are forgiven—because of her great love. Little is forgiven the one whose love is small." He said to her then, "Your sins are forgiven" (Lk 7:47-49). Be kind to one another, compassionate, and mutually forgiving, just as God has forgiven you in Christ (Ep 4:32). Because you are God's chosen ones, holy and beloved, clothe yourselves with heartfelt mercy. . . . Bear with one another, forgive whatever grievances you have against one another. Forgive as the Lord has forgiven you (Col 3:12-13).

God forgives those who forgive (Mt 6:12; Jm 2:13). We can scarcely claim to have been forgiven ourselves if we close our hearts to the forgiveness our brother or sister has need of. Do we close our hearts, or are we prompt to forgive?

The cause of, the reason for, the loving forgiveness which we are to grant one another is the love of God for us—the God-who-is-Love (1 Jn 4:7-21). Are we hard-hearted? Are we unjust, expecting others to have compassion for our failings and not being compassionate ourselves? Do we see the mote in the eye of another, and overlook the beam in our own (Mt 7:3-5).

A patient, merciful imitation of Christ should move us to forgive. How much greater were his sufferings than any we could ever have! And yet, from the cross, he was able to say: "Father, forgive them; they do not know what they are doing" (Lk 23:34). Saint Stephen, the Church's first martyr, imitated Jesus literally. As he was being stoned to death he cried out, "Lord, do not hold this sin against them" (Ac 7:60).

And we—are we capable of suffering as Jesus did, and of forgiving, with him, as he did? Have we made an effort to endure affronts in good part, so as not actually to *need* to be constantly "forgiving someone"? In other words, have we overcome some of our sensitivity? Does our pride present an obstacle to our forgiveness of others?

Have we ourselves offended our neighbor: our spouse, our children, our friends? Do we pray, or go to Mass, without having sought forgiveness of the brother or sister who "has something against us"—or without having accorded our own forgiveness to someone who has offended us (Mt 5:23-24)?

19. Fortitude

Fortitude is that firmness and steadfastness that banishes fear, overcomes all the dangers that make steadfastness extremely difficult, and steers a middle course between timidity and temerity.

> You are forewarned, beloved brothers. Be on your guard lest you be led astray by the error of the wicked, and forfeit the security you enjoy (2 P 3:17). Stay sober and alert. Your opponent the devil is prowling like a roaring lion looking for someone to devour. Resist him, solid in your faith, realizing that the brotherhood of believers is undergoing the same sufferings throughout the world (1 P 5:8-9). "Blest are those persecuted for holiness' sake; the reign of God is theirs" (Mt 5:10). Love is patient. . . . Love does not rejoice in what is wrong, but rejoices with the truth. There is no limit to love's forebearance, to its trust, its hope, its power to endure (1 Cor 13:4, 6-7).

Fortitude's mission is to combat the forces of evil, now by resisting, now by attacking. Are we strong in our capacity for resistance, for standing firm, even though our very fortitude shows us our vulnerability? An essential ingredient of fortitude is *patience*. Do we know how to be patient in time of trial (Jm 1:2-4; 1 Cor 4:12)? Have we become downcast at the onset of misfortune?

But let us not think that patience is a passive virtue. It imitates Christ. As Saint Thomas Aquinas says, "The patient person is not the one who flees evil, but the one who steadfastly confronts, by his or her presence, a disordered state of sorrowfulness." Have we lost our peace and tranquillity of soul at seeing ourselves having to suffer evil for doing good? Do we cloak ourselves in a garment of patience in order to suffer well (Col 3:12), as did the Prophets (Jm 5:10)? Are we too passive in our patience?

In order to have the virtue of fortitude, it is necessary to perform an act of labor, or toil—that toil which transforms us into "good soldiers of

Christ'' who know how to suffer in his cause (2 Tm 2:3, 9). Are we hard-working, or are we slothful, when it comes to resisting evil?

Further: fortitude cannot be acquired by a single act. *Perseverance* is required, so as not to "grow despondent in the struggle" (Heb 12:1-3; Jm 1:6-8; Mt 10:22, 14:13). Do we "drown in a glass of water"? Do we flag in our task when difficulties arise? Do we persevere, knowing that growth takes time, or do we jettison our whole cargo at the sight of the first reef? Do we confuse fortitude with stubbornness?

Can any *fear* disturb us, when we know that nothing, and no one, is stronger than God who keeps our soul from all danger (Mt 10:28; Lk 12:4-5; 1 P 3:14)? Are we fearful? Do we refuse to "get involved" and offer witness when the odds are against us?

20.   Freedom

Freedom is the natural faculty human beings have of acting in one way rather than another or of not acting at all. Hence their responsibility for their deeds. For a Christian, freedom is the ability to perform good works, in the knowledge of the truth and the rejection of sin, as we freely choose God, who has freely chosen us first.

> "The spirit of the Lord is upon me. . . . He has sent me . . . to proclaim liberty to captives . . . and release to prisoners" (Lk 4:18). But now that you are freed from sin and have become slaves of God, your benefit is sanctification as you tend toward eternal life (Rm 6:22). The law of the spirit, the spirit of life in Christ Jesus, has freed you from the law of sin and death (Rm 8:2). The Lord is the Spirit, and where the Spirit of the Lord is, there is freedom (2 Cor 3:17). It was for liberty that Christ freed us. So stand firm, and do not take on yourselves the yoke of slavery a second time! . . . Remember that you have been called to live in freedom—but not a freedom that gives free rein to the flesh. Out of love, place yourselves at one another's service (Gal 5:1, 13).

Freedom is not "doing what I like," it is "doing what I should." Accordingly, "what I like" ought to be the good I should do. Am I really free? That is, do I do good works? Do I realize that sanctity, holiness, consists in the highest degree of freedom? Do I endeavor to conquer the liberty I have received as a gift?

Have I appreciated in depth the Messianic prophecy fulfilled by

Christ: "The spirit of the Lord . . . has sent me . . . to proclaim liberty to captives . . . and release to prisoners"?

Have I reflected on the Christian vocation as a "call to freedom" (Gal 5:13), and the fact that this freedom consists in living in grace, rejecting sin, and being God's slave (Rm 6:22; 2 Cor 3:17)?

Do I realize that to live in sin is to live in slavery, in the false "liberty" of libertinism and license (Gal 5:13-26; 2 P 2:18-19; Rm 6:15; 2 Tm 2:25-26)?

Am I imperious and authoritarian? Do I refuse to permit my spouse, my children, my relatives, my friends, to have their freedom? Am I possessive, enslaving my neighbor to my opinion, taste, or mood of the day? Do I always seek to impose my ideas, while denying my neighbor the freedom and right to have his or her own ideas?

Do I have freedom of spirit (Mt 11:28-30; Jn 3:6-8, 4:23-24, 14:26, 16:13; 2 Cor 3:17; Ep 6:5-7; Col 3:22-24)—or is my life dependent on "what people might say" (the pressures the world would like to place on me) or on my passions?

21. Friendship

Friendship is pure and disinterested affection among persons, generally reciprocal, springing from and fostered by familiarity.

"You are my friends if you do what I command you" (Jn 15:14). O you unfaithful ones, are you not aware that love of the world is enmity to God? A man is marked out as God's enemy if he chooses to be the world's friend (Jm 4:4).

Evidently there are different kinds of friendship, as we can see from the readings. We must discern, on this earth, whether our concept of friendship is the same as God's. Do we do so?

Have we occasionally been unjust toward our friends, treating them as strangers and being unfaithful to the bonds of friendship that unite us? Have we betrayed their confidences, and thereby the charity we should bear them?

Abraham was called the "Friend of God," because of his faith, his trust, and his justice. Do we prize these same things in friendship among human beings? Are they the sole motives of our friendship with others, or do we have "friends of convenience"—friends for profit, friends for use, instead of friends to share with and to serve?

As Scripture says one who has found a friend has found a treasure. But friends are treasures that have to be cared for, and built up, as genuine talents and gifts. Do we cultivate our friends in depth, purifying our common friendship, or do we let our friendship lie untended and fruitless? That is, are we content with a shallow superficial relationship?

Respect, patience, availability, openness to dialogue, appreciation and admiration, trust and disinterest—these are some of the pillars of Christian friendship. Are they pillars of ours?

22. Gratitude

Gratitude is a sense of appreciation for a benefit or favor received or to be received, coupled with a sense of obligation to be worthy of it in some way.

> Whatever you do, whatever in speech or in action, do it in the name of the Lord Jesus. Give thanks to God the Father through him (Col 3:17). Give my greetings to Prisca and Aquila; they were my fellow workers in the service of Christ Jesus and even risked their lives for the sake of mine. Not only I but all the churches of the Gentiles are grateful to them (Rm 16:3-4). He rescued us from the danger of death and will continue to do so. We have put our hope in him who will never cease to deliver us. But you must help us with your prayers, so that on our behalf God may be thanked for the gift granted us through the prayers of so many (2 Cor 1:10-11). Following Paul's summons to the bar, Tertullus began his prosecution by addressing Felix: "Your Excellency, through your efforts we enjoy great peace. Many improvements have been made in this nation through your provident care. Therefore we must always and everywhere acknowledge our deep gratitude to you (Ac 24:2-3).

Jesus had cured ten lepers. Only one returned to thank him (Lk 17:16-19).

We should be thankful, first of all, for the gifts we have received from God. Are we thankful for the gifts of faith, hope, and charity? Are we thankful for the life we have received from God? Are we thankful that our parents have had us baptized, making us sons and daughters of the Church?

But we should also be thankful for the things our brothers and sisters do for us (Rm 16:1-5); Ph 4:15-18; 2 Tm 1-16). Are we? Or do we think that others are supposed to do us favors? Are we grateful to our parents? Are we grateful to our teachers? Have we been guilty of the injustice of ingratitude?

23. Holiness

Holiness is the quality of being perfect and without fault. It is predicated properly in God alone, who is holy by essence, and by grace, privilege, and participation, of the angels and human beings.

"God who is mighty has done great things for me, holy is his name" (Lk 1:49). (I use the following example from human affairs because of your weak human nature.) "Just as formerly you enslaved your bodies to impurity and licentiousness for their degradation, make them now the servants of justice for their sanctification" (Rm 6:19). Since we have these promises, beloved, let us purify ourselves from every defilement of flesh and spirit, and in the fear of God strive to fulfill our consecration perfectly (2 Cor 7:1). You must lay aside your former way of life and the old self. ... Put on that new man created in God's image, whose justice and holiness are born of truth (Ep 4:22, 24). She will be saved through childbearing, provided she continues in faith and love and holiness—her chastity being taken for granted (1 Tm 2:15). They disciplined us as seemed right to them, to prepare us for the short span of mortal life; but God does so for our true profit, that we may share his holiness (Heb 12:10).

As we read in our definition, holiness belongs essentially to God. But he has willed to share himself with us. We participate in him as he is in himself. Thus God's holiness is communicable, and actually communicated, to human beings.

Have we thought about this? Do we wish to have our Lord make us saints? Do we ask him to do so? Do we have the idea that holiness is something reserved to the canonized saints we venerate in pictures and statues, or do we think of it as our own vocation?

Do we realize that God wishes us to be saints, to be holy, and that our food and drink ought to be to do the will of our Father, as it was for Christ (Jn 4:34)?

"Holiness" means "consecration, dedication," or the state of being set apart for God. Have we ever considered that, in virtue of our consecration in baptism, we have been transformed into *saints*, members of a *Holy People*? What became of this sanctity, the holiness, which was poured out upon us in that moment?

Do we pray frequently to the *holy Father*, the *Sanctifier* who makes us holy, that his power may fill our hearts with the Love that proceeds from the Father and the Son?

Do we understand *sacrilege* as an offense to a consecrated person, place, or thing (1 Cor 3:17; Mt 21:13, 7:6; 1 Tm 1:9; Ac 19:37)? Have we ever sinned against God's holiness by receiving Communion in the state of mortal sin? Have we ever considered that, in doing so, we sin against that Temple of God which is ourselves, as well as against the Body and Blood of Christ which we receive unworthily? Have we contracted matrimony without being in the state of God's grace at the time? Have we made unworthy use of sacred things or places desecrating them with our words or actions? Have we used them for superstitious rituals that offend against the proper worship which the Church offers God?

Do we desire that God, the Holy One, be ever hallowed by all men and women (Mt 6:9)?

24. Hope

Hope is the theological virtue by which we firmly trust that God will bestow on us what he has promised. It is the determined course of the human being on his and her pilgrimage toward the Supreme Good.

The grace of God has appeared, offering salvation to all men. It trains us to reject godless ways and worldly desires, and live temperately, justly, and devoutly in this age as we await our blessed hope, the appearing of the glory of the great God and of our Savior Christ Jesus (Tt 2:11-13). But when the kindness and love of God our savior appeared, he saved us; not because of any righteous deeds we had done, but because of his mercy. . . . that we might be justified by his grace and become heirs, in hope, of eternal life, You can depend on this to be true (Tt 3:4-8). For here we have no lasting city; we are seeking one which is to come (Heb 13:14). In hope we were saved. But hope is not hope if its object is seen; how is it possible for one to hope for what he sees? And hoping for what we cannot see means awaiting it with patient endurance (Rm 8:24-25).

"Hope," in Sacred Scripture, is often synonymous with trust, security, and constancy.

Only in God and in his mighty arm can we place our hope. He is himself the object of his promises, the Supreme Good, and it is to him we tend and the possession of him that we long for. We are judged on our hope in his promise (Heb 16:6). Do we truly long to possess the Supreme Good, or do we absolutize the relative goods of this world, thinking them to be *the* things to have?

A joyful hope enables us to stand firm in time of trial (Rm 12:12), since when all other doors are closed, one remains open: the door of hope.

Hope is a theological virtue that goes hand in hand with patience and fortitude—for until we attain to the object of our hope, we live in the midst of struggle (2 Cor 4:8). Do we live and struggle as men and women of hope?

Hope placed in God purifies our desires and intentions (1 Jn 3:3), so that everything we seek, we seek for God.

Often we sin against hope by *presumption* (Lk 18:9, 14; 1 Cor 4:4; Mt 7:21). Presumption is an unnatural, premature anticipation of the fulfillment of our hope, whereby we believe our own strength to be sufficient to gain heaven and the forgiveness of our sins. Another form of presumption is to be so certain that the merits of Christ have saved us that we do nothing on our own part to save ourselves and attain to the Kingdom.

Are we "presumptuous"? That is, do we assign a false value to our own "I," by inordinately affirming the strength of our will, and by being inappropriately sure of ourselves—self-conceited—and lacking in humility as we stand before the gifts of God? As Saint Augustine tells us, "Only to the humble is it given to hope." Are we humble in our hope?

Another sin against hope is that of *despair*—to believe that we have no one to intercede for us (1 Jn 2:1-2). Despair, in the words of Josef Pieper, is the "anti-natural anticipation of non-fulfillment." Saint Isidore of Seville wrote: "Despair is a descent into hell."

Do we doubt of eternal life? Do we oppose Christ's decision to save us? Do we reject the path to the fullness of life? Do we live in that torn

condition of despair which consists in longing no longer—finding no
more reason for living and hoping? Have we fallen into an apathetic sloth,
so that we no longer avail ourselves of the means to cooperate in the work
of hope, the work of our salvation, because we lack greatness of spirit and
the joy of God? Does my spirit rest in God? Can I say, at every moment,
with Christ on the Cross, "Father, into your hands I commend my spirit"
(Lk 23:46)?

There is no better way to live in hope than to abandon ourselves to the
Providence, the "foresight," of a God who knows what we need and who
"provides" for these needs (Mt 6:25-30). Do we seek the Kingdom of
God and his justice, in hope, knowing that all things besides will be given
to us as a bonus (Mt 6:32-34)? Do we not, on the contrary, more usually
hide from the God who seeks us?

25. Hospitality

Hospitality is the virtue we practice toward pilgrims, the needy, the
infirm, and generally all persons, as we open to them our hearts, our
homes, and our goods.

"The king will say to those on his right: 'Come, you have my
Father's blessing! . . . I was a stranger and you welcomed me' "
(Mt 25:34-35). In the vicinity of that place was the estate of
Publius, the chief figure on the island. He took us in and gave us
kind hospitality for three days (Ac 28:7). Your love must be
sincere. . . . Look on the needs of the saints as your own; be
generous in offering hospitality (Romans 12:9, 13). Do not neglect
to show hospitality, for by that means some have entertained angels
without knowing it (Heb 13:2). Be mutually hospitable without
complaining (1 P 4:9).

Hospitality is a manner of loving. It consists in sharing with others the
gift of our openness and liberality.

The Gospel shows us many examples of this hospitality-in-charity
(Lk 10:38-42, 19:1-10, as well as of people's inhospitality toward Jesus
(Lk 9:52-55). Do we *invite Jesus* to come into our heart and into our
home?

But this hospitality is not to be a complaining one (1 P 4:9). Rather it
is to be an obliging one (Rm 12:13). Do we protest if we have to invite
someone to lodge with us? Is it "too much of a bother"? Do we

appreciate that what we do for one of our brothers or sisters is done for Christ, and that what we refuse our brothers or sisters we refuse Christ (Mt 25:35, 43)? Do we expect to have people be hospitable toward ourselves, and then refuse to be hospitable with others?

We have a right to the privacy and intimacy our family needs to have, of course. But beyond this, are our homes not frequently "ghettos"   too closed to others, and hence poor examples of Christian witness and hospitality?

26. Humility

Humility is the Christian virtue which consists in a knowledge of our lowliness and misery, coupled with action in conformity with this knowledge.

"Take my yoke upon your shoulders and learn from me, for I am gentle and humble of heart. Your souls will find rest, for my yoke is easy and my burden light" (Mt 11:29). Just then the disciples came up to Jesus with the question, "Who is of greatest importance in the kingdom of God?" He called a little child over and stood him in their midst and said: "I assure you, unless you change and become like little children, you will not enter the kingdom of God. Whoever makes himself lowly, becoming like this child, is of greatest importance in that heavenly reign" Mt 18:1-4). "Some who are last will be first and some who are first will be last" (Lk 13:30). "For everyone who exalts himself shall be humbled and he who humbles himself shall be exalted" (Lk 14:11). Then he poured water into a basin and began to wash his disciples' feet and dry them with the towel he had around him (Jn 13:5). In the same way, you younger men must be obedient to the elders. In your relations with one another, clothe yourselves with humility, because God "is stern with the arrogant but to the humble he shows kindness." Bow humbly under God's mighty hand, so that in due time he may lift you high (1 P 5:5-6).

The teachings of our Lord and the Apostles with respect to humility are very extensive. This virtue is the contrary of pride, haughtiness, and vanity. It is an aid to temperance.

Jesus appears as "meek," or gentle, and humble of heart (Mt 11:29); Mary sings to the Lord, "He looked upon his servant in her lowliness"

(Lk 1:48); rejoices that he has exalted the lowly (Lk 1:52). Do we glory in the fact that we are exalted if we are humble? Are we humiliated, disturbed, if we are "of humble circumstances" (Jm 1:9)?

Our Lord gives his grace to the humble (1 P 5:5), and exhorts us to this same littleness (1 P 3:8). Do we love to "stand out from the crowd"? Or do we recognize that God works his deeds of grandeur—does great things within us—*only* if we humbly offer him our poverty?

Do we seek to have the first places, forgetting that whoever exalts himself or herself will be humbled, will be brought low (Mt 23:12)? Are we vain, and envious of others' greatness (Gal 5:26). If so, do we make a serious effort to convert ourselves from these attitudes?

Do we "act out of rivalry or conceit," or do we "think humbly of others as superiors" (Ph 2:3)? Are we victims of that worldly mentality that looks down upon humility as stupidity? Or on the contrary, do we consider this virtue to be the basis for a life according to the truth of the Gospel? Does it disturb us when our shortcomings are criticized or judged, or when we are subjected to "fraternal correction"?

27. Illness

Illness is any diminution in the state of our physical or mental health.

Those whom he cured, who were variously afflicted, were many, and so were the demons he expelled. But he would not permit the demons to speak, because they knew him (Mk 1:34). Because he had cured many, all who had afflictions kept pushing toward him to touch him (Mk 3:10).

This subject is closely connected with sin, death, misfortune, and pain.

Jesus bore our infirmities, bore our weakness (Mt:8:17), and became the physician of our bodies and souls. It is from within a state of infirmity that we must discover Christ our Health.

On countless occasions Jesus confronted illnesses as someone having power and authority over them. And indeed he healed them (Mk 5:25-34; Lk 13:11-12; Jn 5:1-9, 9:35; Mt 17:16-18).

The root cause of all sickness is sin. Accordingly, infirmity is a symbol of our condition as weak sinners.

But illness will serve God's plan, or it will not, depending on whether we accept it with faith or not—depending on whether we reject it, or see it as having a redemptive dimension as a price we are invited to pay.

Do I bear the infirmities God permits with joy and hope (Jm 1:2-4)? Am I wise in my infirmities—that is, do I bear the trials of my suffering by directing my gaze beyond the misfortune (Jm 1:12)? Do I realize that sickness and infirmity cannot come directly from the will of God—for God is the author of all good (Jm 1:13-18)—but that God sometimes permits it in order to achieve a greater good, or even, on rare occasions as a punishment (Lk 1:20-22)? Do I know that illness, suffered and accepted in good part, can purify me of my sins and save others as well?

Our Lord was accustomed to say, "Go and sin no more," or "Give up your sins (Jn 5:5-14). Do I realize that a sinless life is a "positive negation" of the evil of illness and infirmity? Do I recognize the importance of faith not only for my spiritual health, but for my physical and mental health as well (Mt 9:12)?

The Sacrament of the Sick is not the sacrament of the dying, but the sacrament of consolation for those who are ill. Have I sought this sacrament for my relatives when they were seriously ill, or have I deprived them of this boon so as not to "scare" them? When faced with physical pain, have I resented God—forgetting Jesus' pain and suffering? Do we practice the work of mercy that consists in visiting and caring for the sick (Mt 25:36)? Are we patient with them?

28. Inebriation

Inebriation is a temporary incapacitation of the faculties due to excessive consumption of alcoholic beverages.

> "If the servant is worthless and . . . begins . . . to eat and drink with drunkards, that man's master will return when he is not ready and least expects him. He will punish him severely and settle with him as is done with hypocrites" (Mt 24 48-51). "Be on your guard lest your spirits become bloated with indulgence and drunkenness and worldly cares. The great day will suddenly close in on you like a trap" (Lk 21:34). No . . . drunkards . . . will inherit God's kingdom (1 Cor 6:9-10). Avoid getting drunk on wine; that leads to debauchery. Be filled with the Spirit . . . (Ep 5:18).

God's Word invites us to temperance (1 Th 5:6; 2 Tm 1:7), and a sober, religious life (Tt 2:12-13).

There is a close relationship between "dulling the mind" and being too casual about certain excesses—in this case, the excessive consumption of alcohol. Moderation and due proportion should guide our conduct here.

This sin will not always consist in being constantly intoxicated. One can be an alcoholic without being the town "drunk."

Leaving aside any consideration of the fact that I may have the disease of alcoholism, let me ask myself the following questions: Am I sober in my use of alcohol? Do I frequently drink to excess? Am I "macho" in my drinking habits—do I drink to show what a "man" I am? Do I drink to "drown my sorrows"? Do I consider the serious damage I am doing to myself and my family? Do I realize that I could be giving scandal to the people who look to me for a good example, and who need this good example? Do I refuse medical assistance even though I know I am dependent on alcohol? If I have ever been, or thought I was, intoxicated—what do I think Christ thought of me at this moment. The answer to this question should be of interest and importance to me.

29. Jealousy

Jealousy is the anxious, mistrustful suspicion that someone I love may have transferred, or be transferring, his or her affection to someone else.

> It is obvious what proceeds from the flesh: lewd conduct . . . jealousy, outbursts of rage, selfish rivalries . . . (Gal 5:19-20).

Jealousy always contains a heavy dose of subjectivism and diffidence. We could almost say that diffidence—mistrust of self—is the very basis of jealousy.

Especially in the case of married persons and persons keeping company, jealousy tends to be accompanied by constant anxiety and preoccupation. And as the jealousy increases, so does a great animosity toward the other person, based on an attitude of exclusive possession.

Jealousy is an attitude altogether at variance with the teaching of Christ, according to which we ought to be living in trust, peace, and freedom—the very things jealousy kills. Have we ever examined in depth our motives for our jealousy in dialogue with the person who is the object of that jealousy? Does jealousy not imply a certain immaturity, a certain refusal to accord my fellow human beings their freedom—usually along with risky or rash judgments and interpretations of the facts, all in a spirit of consummate superficiality?

30. Joy

Joy is a pleasant, animated, jubilant movement of the spirit, whether for happy and gladsome cause, or, at times, without evident cause, and generally manifested exteriorily.

"Nevertheless, do not rejoice so much in the fact that the devils are subject to you as that your names are inscribed in heaven" (Lk 10:20). "As the father has loved me, so I have loved you. Live on in my love. You will live in my love if you keep my commandments, even as I have kept my Father's commandments, and live in his love. All this I tell you that my joy may be yours and your joy may be complete" (Jn 15:9-11). "Ask and you shall receive, that your joy may be full" (Jn 16:24). Now, however, I come to you; I say all this while I am still in the world that they may share my joy completely" (Jn 17:13).

We should be cheerful, joyous givers (2 Cor 9:6-7), as Saint Paul teaches us, echoing the Book of Proverbs.

But what actually happens? Do we not sometimes give sorrowfully, almost as if we regretted giving the gift or granting the favor? If so . . . we are regretting having done what Christ would have done in the same situation!

Generally our joy and gladness is linked to our well-being or good fortune. But Christ teaches us, in his personal testimony as well as later, in the Apostolic teaching, that we ought not to lose our interior joy even in the midst of tribulations (Jm 1:2-12; Heb 1:9, 10:34; 1 Th 1:6; Col 1:24; Ph 2:17; 2 Cor 6:10, 7:4).

We shall have *certitude* that our sorrow will be transformed into gladness (Jn 16:20), if we place our hope in Jesus' resurrection and our own *which pass by way of his death and ours*, and do not doubt that the true "land" of joy is in heaven (1 P 1:4-6, 8-9).

Are we filled with joy when dealing with the things of God, as the disciples were when they saw the Lord (Jn 20:20)? Are we filled with joy when we do works of mercy (Rm 12:8) and see how happy we are making others?

Our one sorrow must be at not being saints. This sorrow will be a goad and incentive to our conversion. "Worldly sorrow brings death" (2 Cor 7:10). Now this deep sadness the world has—will it not perhaps be on account of a loss of hope, a failure to look at things through new eyes, the eyes of Jesus? Are we guilty of this failure?

Do we infect our neighbor with joy, or with this "worldly sorrow"? Whichever of the two we carry in our heart, this is the one that will be "contagious."

31. Justice

Justice is the constant, unalterable will to render "to each his own"—to render to every person what is his or hers by right.

> "Seek first his kingship over you, his way of holiness, and all these things will be given you besides" (Mt 6:33). "Blest are they who hunger and thirst for holiness; they shall have their fill" (Mt 5:6). It would have been better for them not to have recognized the road to holiness than to have turned their backs on the holy law handed on to them, once they had known it (2 P 2:21). On the contrary, in all that we do we strive to present ourselves as ministers of God . . . with the message of truth and the power of God; wielding the weapons of righteousness with right hand and left . . . (2 Cor 6:4, 7). The kingdom of God is not a matter of eating or drinking, but of justice, peace, and the joy that is given by the Holy Spirit (Rm 14:17).

Justice is a "social virtue." Its purpose, Saint Thomas Aquinas tells us, is "to order the human being in what is called his and her relationship to the other"—that is, justice seeks the good of the other—"while the other virtues are limited to the perfecting of the human being as considered solely in himself and herself."

Am I unjust, neglecting to look to the other, and failing to render what is his or her due?

Every sin is in some way an injustice. Here, however, our concern is to examine justice and injustice in their more proper sense.

It is an injustice to award *public offices and functions* by favoritism. In view of the dignity and importance to the common good of holding public office, such posts ought to be conferred upon persons who are more worthy of and suitable for them. Have we taken this into account when and if it has fallen to us to participate in such conferral? Or have we been moved by ''influence,'' and ''recommendations''?

It is likewise unjust to fail to pay our employees a *just wage*. This is a sin that ''cries aloud'' (Jm 5:4). One even finds instances where employers pay less than the legal minimum wage. Are we guilty here? If so, are we endeavoring to put an end to this situation? Are we aware that the legal minimum wage is precisely a *minimum*? Sometimes we seem to think of it as a maximum.

Do we treat those who serve us—our employees, our household help, and so on—with respect and consideration (Col 4:1), or are we unjust with them (1 Cor 6:8-9)?

With regard to the *payment of taxes* (Lk 20:22-25, Rm 13:1-7)—do we do so punctually and ''integrally,'' or do we fall into the trap popular opinion sets for us and think we have to evade and lie? After all, we say, the government knows about tax evasion, and simply raises the percentage to cover the difference. Why should I pay more than everybody else? (But who started the vicious circle, the government or the evaders?)

Sometimes people consider tax laws to be ''merely penal'' laws. That is, we consider that there is no *moral* obligation to pay them, unless we are ''caught'' and specifically directed to pay—somewhat as we consider that we are not *morally* obliged to stop at a traffic sign ''out in the middle of nowhere,'' but only to pay the fine if we are apprehended. But in the case of taxes, this principle applies only to certain customs taxes at most. For the rest, let us limit it to traffic regulations (and not all of these), where it belongs. If we practice tax evasion, this will make the taxes imposed by the state unjust, for the law of just proportion and equity, which considers the ability and economic circumstances of the citizens, will fall into disuse.

Our Lord tells us that it is unjust to *judge*. Obviously this does not refer to any and every type of judgment—for instance, our Lord does not forbid us to correct our brothers' and sisters' faults, provided we do so with kindness. What is forbidden is self-righteousness, contempt, and rash judgment (judgment based on unfounded suspicion). Are we guilty?

It is a matter of justice conscientiously to carry out the obligations of our *personal employment or other contractual engagements*, as well as *social duties* imposed on us by the common good.

It is likewise a matter of justice to impose *just punishment* for crimes, misdemeanors, malfeasance, or other delinquencies. But in order to be just, a punishment must be proportioned to the malice of the transgression. Have we erred here, either by excess or by defect?

It is an injustice to bear *false testimony*. It is likewise an obligation in justice to come to the aid of individuals by testifying in their behalf, both for the good of society, and in order to deliver an innocent person from unjust injury. Have we avoided testifying in court—for instance when we have witnessed a traffic accident—because we "didn't want to be bothered"?

It is a most serious fault against justice to *attack the life, physical integrity, or material or spiritual goods of one's neighbor, to impugn his or her reputation and honor, or to deprive one's neighbor of his or her freedom.*

These are *human rights*, and they touch upon the most intimate aspects of human life.

Have I violated human rights? Seriously? Have I caused irreparable damage in this respect? Have I associated with groups that make use of torture, or other illegal constraints and oppression?

Usury, in olden times, merely meant taking interest on a loan. Modern economic laws see nothing illicit in this reimbursement for the use of capital, within certain limits. But the investment of capital, in enterprises which make large profits without paying just wages, or by changing unjustly high prices, can be usury in the morally reprehensible sense. That is, it becomes a way of making money produce more than it ought to.

It is a grave fault against justice to *exploit a human being* (Lk 15:15-17, 20:47; 1 Cor 6:8; Jm 5:1-6; 1 Tm 6:9-10; Gal 5:15; 1 Th 4:6). Do we utilize persons unjustly, instead of serving them in justice? Do we treat woman as a mere object of pleasure (1 P 3:3-6). Do we have a "classist" mentality, which is so attached to material goods that it exploits other classes in order to have more (Lk 9:49-50, 16:19-31, Mk 10:17, 22)?

It is a matter of justice to *make restitution*—to "restore the unjustly retained goods of another, or to repair unjustly caused material or moral damage.'' Restitution comes down to not injuring the rights of another (Mt 22:21; Lk 19:8; Rm 13:7; Jm 5:4). When we go to confession, do we simply accuse ourselves of "taking things," or of "faults against justice," without any intention of restoring the things taken? Do we make restitution when we have injured another's reputation by our detraction or calumny?

Joseph Pieper, the well-known modern Catholic philosopher and theologian, tells us: "The most wicked corruption of the natural order in the human realm, the most authentic perversion of the 'common weal,' is called by the name of 'injustice.' "

Do we appreciate the nature and gravity of this disorder? Do we observe the ancient law of justice which says, "Do not unto others as we would not have others do unto us, but do unto others as we would have others do unto us"? Any other way of conducting ourselves is injustice: it means applying a broad standard in my own case, and a strict standard for my neighbor.

Are we capable of observing the natural law of the *secret*—or have we violated this law by divulging (even "in confidence") what others have told us in confidence? Have we read other people's correspondence, thereby delving into intimacies they would not have wished to share with us?

Just as we are bound to our parents by obligations of "filial piety"— the loyalty of sons and daughters—so there is another kind of "piety," or loyalty, called *patriotism*, which binds us to our country. But we must also know that this patriotism should keep us far removed from attitudes and behavior which actually oppose genuine patriotism. At one extreme, of course, is that pretended "universal love" (actually, an abstract "love") for "humanity" which somehow seems to exclude love for actual human beings, so that in loving the "whole" world we end up by loving neither our own country nor the *real* world. But at the other extreme, there are those who lock themselves up in a blind nationalism that leads them to believe that, in order to love their own country, they have to hate other peoples' countries.

Are we negligent of our duties in justice toward our country, or of the respect we owe those who govern it—which duties, and respect, do not exclude our duties of charity, benevolence, and respect toward the countries of others?

Do we realize that, after God and our parents, it is to our country that we owe the most? Do we practice the "piety," or loyalty—the patriotism—that this calls for?

32. Love

Love is that movement of the will by which we seek our real or imagined good and endeavor to enjoy it. As Christian charity, love consists in that movement of benevolence-in-action with which God has loved us, and which enables us to love Him above all things, and our neighbor, in Him, as ourselves.

> "Yes, God so loved the world that he gave his only Son, that whoever believes in him may not die but have eternal life" (Jn 3:16). Jesus said to him: " 'You shall love the Lord your God with your whole heart, and with your whole soul, and with all your mind.'' This is the greatest and first commandment. The second is like it: 'You shall love your neighbor as yourself.' On these two commandments the whole law is based, and the prophets as well'' (Mt 22:37-38). "As the Father has loved me, so I have loved you. Live on in my love. You will live in my love if you keep my commandments, even as I have kept my Father's commandments, and live in his love. . . . This is my commandment: love one another as I have loved you. There is no greater love than this: to lay down one's life for one's friends" (Jn 15:9-10, 12-13). "Were God your father you would love me, for I came forth from God, and am here. I did not come of my own will; it was he who sent me" (Jn 8:42). "I give you a new commandment: Such as my love has been for you, so must your love be for each other. This is how all will know you for my disciples: your love for one another" (Jn 13:34-35). "Love your enemy and do good; lend without expecting repayment. Then will your recompense be great. You will rightly be called sons of the Most High, since he himself is good to the ungrateful and the wicked. Be compassionate, as your Father is compassionate" (Lk 6:35-36).

This broad subject is treated in many places in Sacred Scripture, where it is synonymous with charity, affection, tenderness, compassion, benevolence, mercy, goodness, and understanding. Each of the passages we have selected can suggest conclusions for our examination of conscience.

To love God with all our being is the greatest and first commandment (Mt 22:37-38; Mk 12:30). It has no equal. Without love and charity for God, the Cause and Origin of all love, all good, and all truth, we cannot rightly love either our neighbor or ourselves. Have we often thought about God's *personal reality*? Or do we somehow think of him as a "Being," less real than the creatures we see around us hence not the prime object of our love?

To love God *before* and *more than* anyone else is a duty of justice in the face of an observable experience: God has loved us first (1 Jn 4:9), and it is by His benevolent love that we exist. Are we grateful and loving in view of this gift of the initiative of God's charity, with which He first conceived us in loving thought, and then, with the same love, fashioned us from nothing?

When we are shaken and crushed by suffering, God's love seems to be silent as if he had abandoned us. After all, we reason if God is love, he cannot send evil upon his creatures. Here Saint Paul's example will encourage and strengthen us. We should ask the same question as he,—and give the same answer. "Who will separate us from the love of Christ?" he cried (Rm 8:35).

Saint Paul, once more, in his Hymn to the Gift of Love (1 Cor 13), teaches us that no work or sacrifice has any value, not even the laying down of one's life, if charity be absent. Do we attempt to evaluate our actions without measuring the degree of love present in them?

There are people who think they can love God without loving their brothers and sisters. Anyone who thinks this is thinking a lie—is thinking something impossible (1 Jn 4:20-21). Do we not sometimes substitute "religion"—a "God" tailored to our needs—for our responsibilities toward our brothers and sisters? Our responsibility is to love them tirelessly, patiently, and thanklessly, "putting ourselves out," and losing our time.

Yet we may not content ourselves even with a love like this— excellent and unattainable as it may seem. Christ asks us to go further still, and love even our enemies (Lk 6:27-28)—to render efficacious, concrete good to those who render us equally efficacious, concrete evil. To love those who love us has little merit. This alone would constitute a step backward and downward, for even evil persons hold someone dear (Mt 5:46).

The problem is not so much a theoretical one as it is a practical one. *How* are we to love?

The answer? By praying for ourselves, that we may be transformed into people in love. By praying for sinners, that they may be converted and live. By praying for the good, that they may abide in justice and love. By giving alms, to relieve ourselves of our superfluities (Lk 11:41, 13:33), since superfluities belong to others. By serving Christ in various works of mercy on behalf of our brother or sister in misery (Mt 25:41-45). By practicing "fraternal correction," since if we are listened to, we shall have "gained our brother" or sister by this deed of love (Mt 18:15).

Are these all things we do? Or on the contrary, do we scandalize our brothers and sisters by our loveless behavior (Mt 18:7, Mk 9:41-42, Rm 14:13)?

Scandal is a word we actually have from the Gospel. It denotes the spiritual damage or ruination we may cause our neighbor. Scripture places us on our guard against those who commit scandal (Mt 18:6-9, 1 P 2:8). Have we considered the injustice and un-love of harming our neighbor by our word or conduct? Have we been the cause of anyone's losing the faith?

The God who is Love can only live where people in love have created a climate or atmosphere in which He can breathe. Whoever abides in love, abides in God, and God dwells in him or her (1 Jn 4:16).

Do we create such an atmosphere and climate around us? Are we tolerant of our neighbor's defects? Do we live in discord? Do we have mercy on the misery of others?

Finally, only love can sweep away the fear and terrors that weigh us down so that we can scarcely creep along (1 Jn 4:18).

Are we afraid to fall in love with the One Who will burst the bonds of our fears?

33. Lying

Lying is any expression contrary to what we know, believe, or think.

"The father you spring from is the devil, and willingly you carry out his wishes. He brought death to man from the beginning, and has never based himself on truth; the truth is not in him. Lying speech is his native tongue; he is a liar and the father of lies" (Jn 8:44). See to it, then, that you put an end to lying; let everyone speak the truth to his neighbor, for we are members of one another (Ep 4:25). Stop lying to one another. What you have done is put aside your old self with its past deeds . . . (Col 3:9). My reason for having written you is not that you do not know the truth but that you do, and that no lie has anything in common with the truth. Who is the liar? He who denies that Jesus is the Christ. He is the antichrist, denying the Father and the Son (1 Jn 2:21-22). Outside are the dogs and sorcerers, the fornicators and murderers, the idol-worshipers and all who love falsehood (Rv 22:15).

Lying is truly an "unnatural" vice, since the human intellect is ordered to a knowledge of the truth of things and to the proclamation of that knowledge.

There are many forms of lying, but each consists in denying what the intellect presents to itself as certain.

Gossip and detraction generally involve a great deal of lying. Rarely do we criticize someone's defects in pious concern for the truth. Nearly always, the delights of gossip, together with our personal antipathies and subjective judgments, lead us to exaggerate our victim's weak points. This is a form of lying (Rm 1:29-32, 2 Cor 12:20). Are we habituated to this sin? Are we fond of casual gossip, the biting word—the lie? Are we unaware that this is a form of injustice?

Rash judgments can simply demolish a person's reputation (Rm 2:1-3, 14:10; Mt 7:1; Lk 6:37; Jn 7:24; Jm 4:12-13). Do we judge according to the truth, or do we judge "rashly"? Do we "generously" pronounce a favorable judgment on someone in order to call attention to unsavory suspicions concerning that person?

Calumny, which is false and lying detraction of someone, when it is in a grave matter, goes to the extreme in offending against the right to a reputation which we all have. It is a form of lying which kills its victim in his or her reputation (Mt 5:11, 1 P 3:16). Are we inclined to the sin of calumny? Have we actually calumniated our neighbor? Upon coming to ourselves, and comprehending the gravity of our act, have we repented of our sin, and made restitution for our theft of a reputation?

Generally speaking, *sins of the tongue* tend to fall into the category of lying. Holy Scripture speaks of the tongue as a "small member" that can start a conflagration, as a tiny spark can start a forest fire (Jm 3:1-18, 1:26; 1 P 2:1-2). Do we "talk too much"? Are we prone to exaggeration and "story telling"—unhappily such a common fault among human beings? Do we speak of ourselves with the same severity and falsehood with which we speak of our neighbor? Should we like to have others speak this way of ourselves?

But we are just the contrary of liars. We are *sons and daughters of the truth*. We have been born to be imitators of the Truth—to follow Him, proclaim Him, and serve Him (Jn 9:20-23, 12:41-43; Mt 22:16; Ep 4:14-15, 6:14; 2 Jn 4; 1 Cor 3:7-8; 2 Cor 6:14; 1 Tm 3:15). Would we give our lives for the truth? Do we love it? Do we cultivate and foster it, keeping it in our heart and on our lips?

One hears of so-called "white lies"—lies which "don't hurt anybody." But every lie "hurts" the truth—hence it "hurts" both the person who tells it and the one who has to listen to it. There is no such thing as a white lie. Sometimes we lie to someone seriously ill. This only defrauds that person of his or her right to know the state of his or her health. We must find a way to tell the patient the truth. It is true that there can be cases in which the truth should be concealed in order to avoid a greater evil, but never at the price of telling an actual lie. *A lie is always evil.*

34.   Obedience

Obedience is docile compliance with the will of a person whom we recognize to have authority over us.

> He went down with them then, and came to Nazareth, and was obedient to them (Lk 2:51). As he moved on he saw Levi the son of Alphaeus at his tax collector's post, and said to him, "Follow me." Levi got up and became his follower (Mk 2:14). And it was thus that he humbled himself, obediently accepting even death, death on a cross! (Ph 2:8). Son though he was, he learned obedience from

what he suffered (Heb 5:8). "Whoever does the will of my heavenly Father is brother and sister and mother to me" (Mt 12:50).

Jesus Christ appears in the Gospels as our model of obedience to the Father (Mt 6:10, 26:39-54; Jn 4:32-34, 5:30, 6:38-40, 15:10) as well as to his fellow human beings: he obeys his parents, as well as duly constituted civil and religious authority (Mt 17:24-27; Lk 2:22-51, 5:4-15), and asks this same obedience of us (Mt 23:2-3; Rm 13:1-5; Ep 6:1, 5-8; 1 P 2:13-17; Col 3:20).

Mary imitates him by an obedience in which she refers to herself as the Lord's "servant" (Lk 1:38, 48, 2:1-5).

In the first Christian communities, the faithful were obedient to the authority of the Apostles (Ac 9:32, 14:36-41, 18:23; 1 Cor 4:1-5; Gal 4:19); and the Apostles required this obedience of them (2 Cor 2:9), praising it (Ph 2:12) as a guarantee of salvation (1 Tm 4:12-16; 2 P 1:20).

But our obedience must not be servile and cringing, self-seeking, and serving its own base interests, but filial, loving, and full of respect (Heb 13:17; 1 Cor 16:10-11; Tt 2:15; 1 Th 5:12-13). Each of us ought to be subject to our brother or sister in obedience, out of fear of the Lord (1 Cor 14:32; Ep 5:21).

Are we obedient? Or do we have a foolish and immature spirit of rebellion that is automatically against everything decided by someone else? Am I obedient to my parents, as Christ was to Mary and Joseph (Ep 6:1-8)? Or on the contrary, do I sadden them with my capricious acts of rebellion? Do I believe that I am affirming my personhood when I disobey my elders, becuse I am showing them that I can do what I want? Is my disobedience a bad example to others, and a cause of discord and division? Is my obedience calculating, servile, pharisaical, and fawning?

Is obedience the guiding norm of my actions (Mt 3:13-16; Jn 13:3-9)? Am I obedient to my vocation as a Christian (Mt 4:18-22; Lk 21:28-31), knowing that it is better to obey God than to obey human beings (Ac 4:19; Rm 1:1), in imitation of Christ, who was always obedient to his Father (Rm 3:25, 5:9; Heb 5:7-8)? Do we obey those placed over us (Heb 13:17), in deed as well as in word, cooperating with them so that they may be successful in the exercise of their authority, and trusting them (Jm 1:19-25)?

35. Penitence, Penance

Penitence is the virtue consisting in sorrow for having sinned and the firm purpose not to sin again. Penance is a series of laborious exercises with which we seek to procure the mortification of our passions and senses in order to satisfy the divine justice.

> "At the judgment, the citizens of Nineveh will rise along with the present generation, and they will condemn it. For at the preaching of Jonah they reformed, but you have a greater than Jonah here" (Lk 11:32). Even now I find my joy in the suffering I endure for you. In my own flesh I fill up what is lacking in the suffering of Christ for the sake of his body, the church (Col 1:24). If we say, "We are free of the guilt of sin," we deceive ourselves; the truth is not to be found in us. But if we acknowledge our sins, he who is just can be trusted to forgive our sins and cleanse us from every wrong (1 Jn 1:8-9). Cleanse your hands, you sinners; purify your hearts, you backsliders. . . . Let your laughter be turned into mourning and your joy into sorrow. Be humbled in the sight of the Lord and he will raise you on high (Jm 4:8-10). The Lord does not delay in keeping his promise—though some consider it "delay." Rather, he shows you generous patience, since he wants none to perish but all to come to repentance (2 P 3:9).

"Penitence," "penance," and "conversion" go together. There is no conversion without actions that help to leave the old self behind, nor is there true penance without the repentance of our sins and a desire to reach God.

Works of penance will not be mere acts of self-purification, as for instance fasting for reasons of physical and mental health alone. Their principal purpose will be to graft us onto Christ our Redeemer, incorporating us into his deed of salvation on the cross, which was his rejection of sin and his obedient "Yes" to the Father.

It would be a great sin to despair of God's goodness. He is forgiveness for those who repent, and express their repentance in sincere acts of penance (1 Jn 2:1-2).

The great "penitential practices" of the ancient Church were prayer, fasting, and alms. Do we practice these forms of charity, by which we imitate our Lord and touch our brother and sister? Is fasting, for us, the purely negative "act" of not eating, or do we give it a social sense by sharing the money we save so that our brother or sister in need may have something to eat? Do I share what I have as an alms with particular individuals, as well as with institutions of social assistance like my parish, shelters, soup kitchens, and so on?

The virtue of penitence is the desire to pay for my sins. It finds perfect and complete expression in the Sacrament of Reconciliation, which was instituted by Christ for the forgiveness of our sins (Jn 20:21-23; Mt 18:11).

Do we celebrate the Sacrament of Penance frequently? Do I make my examination of conscience well and carefully, according to the Gospel's criteria for the reform of one's life? Do I perform the penance imposed upon me intelligently, with a desire to devote myself to the practice of the virtue that is opposite to the vice into which I have fallen? Do I know that the merciful Christ is the propitiation for our sins? Do I recognize the Church and its priestly minister as mediators of the forgiveness which God grants a penitent?

36. Perfection

Perfection is the greatest possible degree of goodness or excellence in a given quality.

"In a word, you must be made perfect as your heavenly Father is perfect" (Mt 5:48). Jesus told him, "If you seek perfection, go, sell your possessions, and give to the poor. You will then have treasure in heaven. Afterward, come back and follow me" (Mt:19-21). We even rejoice when we are weak and you are strong. Our prayer is that you may be built up to completion (2 Cor 13:9). Over all these virtues put on love, which binds the rest together and makes them perfect (Col 3:14). It is he who gave apostles, prophets, evangelists, pastors and teachers in roles of service for the faithful to build up the body of Christ, till we become one in faith and in the knowledge of God's Son, and from that perfect man who is Christ come to full stature (Ep 4:11-13). By one offering he has forever perfected those who are being sanctified (Heb 10:14). It is not that I have reached it yet, or have already finished my course;

but I am racing to grasp the prize if possible, since I have been grasped by Christ Jesus (Ph 3:12).

Human beings live under the law of progress and growth—the law of growing to completeness, the law of perfection. Anyone who flags in the race remains in his or her imperfection—in the state of an unfinished human being.

Christ gives us a commandment: to be perfect as his Father is perfect (Mt 5:42). We know we can never attain to this perfection, but we are keeping the commandment if we *tend* toward it, if we strive toward it and move toward it.

Do we seek to be perfect? Do we live a life of the love of God, who is the source of all perfection? Do we strive to instill this same spirit in others by word and example?

The love of God is acquired by living the obedience Jesus lived—an obedience which took him all the way to death on a cross (1 P 2:21-25). In this act of perfect subjection, Jesus attained his end, his fulfillment, his completeness—his perfection.

Do we obey for love—in order to become perfect in love? Or do we consider obedience as a brake on our personal growth—as an insufferable burden?

In the light of the demands of the Gospel, and without any pridefulness or vainglory, are we anxious to perfect our human gifts and talents, our culture and our spiritual life, so as to manifest God's perfection more clearly in our lives? Or on the contrary, are we negligent, and allow our spirit to flag in the way of true progress? Are we wishy-washy in our thinking and actions, so that we become lukewarm and tepid (Rv 3:16), believing ourselves to be good because we are not excessively evil?

37. Pleasure

Pleasure is a quality attaching to activities insofar as they produce contentment of spirit or an agreeable sensation in the body. It is often used to describe amusements and entertainment.

> Men will be lovers of self . . . treacherous, reckless, pompous, lovers of pleasure rather than of God (2 Tm 3:2, 4). Thinking daytime revelry a delight, they are stain and defilement as they share your feasts in a spirit of seduction (2 P 2:13).

The subject of pleasure is closely connected with that of temperance, of which we shall treat below.

The Scripture texts we have cited refer to extreme cases, Christian teaching, while criticizing these cases, evidently does not forbid us to enjoy legitimate, genuine pleasure. It places us on our guard against *excesses*, against overloading the healthy human capacity for pleasure, relaxation, enjoyment, and recreation.

Our Lord shared feasts and banquets, which without any doubt were a source of pleasure and joy to him (Jn 2:1-12; Mt 9:10, 11:18-19). But we may affirm with the same certitude that even the most pleasurable diversions were not a way of escape for him; rather they were the salubrious, enriching complemental of a normal, balanced life. Is this a description of our own pleasures and entertainments? Or instead, are our minds numbed by the "noise" of pleasures that drown out true dialogue and interpersonal relationships?

Are our celebrations superficial, "worldly," and devoid of any spiritual side? Do we not often move according to laws the "word" imposes on us, by "what people will say," and by what "everybody does"? Do we tolerate wild parties our children attend—or even "throw"? Do we waste other people's money as well as our own, besides risking our children's well being, by such violations of common sense, poverty, and justice? Expensive parties, remember, cost money that is not ours—for no superfluities rightfully belong to their possessor.

Have we sought deep joy in our pleasure and entertainment— pleasures with a higher, more profound, more humane and more humanizing, more personalizing meaning—by choosing forms of recreation that are ordered to noble and dignifying ends?

Let us not forget that even good things are to be used in moderation, and that there are things which, while not evil in themselves, can be inappropriate for a person who is striving for perfection.

Do we know how our children amuse themselves? Do we exercise right judgment and wholesome control in their regard? Do we let them spend their days in front of the television, oblivious of the power of most of the programs on the "tube" either to "brainwash" their viewers or to transform them into idiots?

Do we channel our intelligence toward a wise selection of our motives for pleasure and the means of attaining it?

38.   Prayer

Prayer is praise, thanksgiving, or supplication, vocal or silent, directed to God or the saints.

> "This is how you are to pray: 'Our Father in heaven, hallowed be your name, your kingdom come, your will be done on earth as it is in heaven. Give us today our daily bread, and forgive us the wrong we have done as we forgive those who wrong us. Subject us not to the trial but deliver us from the evil one'" (Mt 6:9-13). "You will receive all that you pray for, provided you have faith" (Mt 21:22). On reaching the place he said to them, "Pray that you may not be put to the test" (Lk 22:40). Dismiss all anxiety from your minds. Present your needs to God in every form of prayer and in petitions full of gratitude (Ph 4:6).

Jesus Christ is himself our example of dedication to prayer (Mt 26:36-44; Mk 1:35; Lk 5:16), both in public and in private (Mt 11:25-26, 14:23, 26:36; Mk 11:25). Prayer, he declares, is the principal force by which his Kingdom will be established (Mt 6:9-10, 9:36-38).

Are there particular moments of the day which we devote to prayer—morning and evening, for example, according to an ancient custom of the Church? Do we say grace both before and after meals?

Jesus teaches us that prayer and mortification, or penance, are more persuasive than words (Mk 9:28-29). Do we redouble our efforts at a life of prayer and voluntary sacrifice during lent and Holy Week?

Do we ask as Jesus asked—conditioning our petition on the will of the Father? Or are we demanding in our prayer (Mt 26:36-46)?

The Apostles and first Christians understood their Teacher's instructions very clearly: they founded praying communities (Lk 24:53; Ac 1:12-14, 2:42-47, 4:23-29, 12:5, 20:36), and the value of prayer stands out in the teaching of the Apostles (Rm 12:12; 1 Th 5:17; Jm 4:3, 5:13-18).

Are we distracted in prayer, rattling off words without any concern about our interior disposition (Mt 6:5, 7)? Do we keep in mind that adoration is an indispensable facet of all good prayers? Do we consider the Our Father as the best of all prayers (Lk 11:1-13), and do we meditate its meaning deeply?

Do we beg God for religious and priestly vocations, vocations to the Church's ministry of evangelization (Mt 9:37-38, Col 4:3, Heb 13:18-19)?

Do we pray with perseverance (Lk 18:1-8), asking our Lord to increase our faith (Lk 17:5), or do we easily become discouraged and weary of prayer?

Do we thank God for the manifold benefits we have received from him (Rm 1:20-21; 1 Tm 4:4-5)? Do we praise him for his greatness (Rm 15:5-6; Rv 4:8-11), and aspire to union with him (2 Cor 5:4)? Do we pray not to fall into temptation (2 Cor 12:8)? Do we pray for all men and women, and especially for those in government (1 Tm 2:1-7)? Do we pray for relief from our sorrow (Jm 5:13)? Do we pray for the wicked, for sinners, and for those who persecute the Church and the just, that they may be converted (Mt 5:44)?

Do we pray with humility (Lk 18:10), in recognition of our misery and littleness, or is our prayer a hymn of self-praise (Lk 18:9-14)? Is our prayer personal and intimate, where the Father sees us in secret (Mt 6:6), or do we like to have others think we are pious and devoted to prayer (Mt 6:5)?

39. Pride

Pride is arrogance, vanity, or an exaggeration of one's own worth, nearly always coupled with a contempt for others and an inordinate desire to be preferred to them.

> Whoever teaches in any other way, not holding to the sound doctrines of our Lord Jesus Christ and the teaching proper to true religion, should be recognized as both conceited and ignorant, a sick man in his passion for polemics and controversy (1 Tm 6:3-4). If anyone thinks he amounts to something, when in fact he is nothing, he is only deceiving himself (Gal 6:3). Who confers any distinction upon you? Name something you have that you have not received. If, then, you have received it, why are you boasting as if it were your own? (1 Cor 4:7).

Pride is treated in many places in Scripture, under the names of-haughtiness, arrogance, bragging and boasting, presumption, and conceit.

In view of Jesus' option for the poor, the weak and those whom the world despises, what cause can we possibly have for being puffed up with pride? Surely we should glory in nothing but the Lord (1 Cor 1:27-29, 31). Are we not in the habit of thinking ourselves something, when actually we are not very much at all (Gal 6:3)?

Have our pride and our appetite for glory and honor frequently made us ambitious, jealous envious, haughty and imperious with our equals?

We ought to have enough humility to see that everything comes from God as a gift, and that we should recognize our talents as being from him (1 Cor 4:7). Is this what we do? Are we thankful and grateful, or do we rather puff ourselves up with our supposed qualities and endowments? Do we love praise? Do we seek it, flaunting our abilities and gifts for all to see?

The only pride which we may be permitted is in the knowledge that we have been chosen by our Lord for his Kingdom. This certitude should motivate us to a humble and filial attitude of praise and thanksgiving. Do we praise God for his greatness—and for having worked mighty deeds in our littleness (Lk 1:48-49)?

In the popular sense of the word, it is surely permitted to be "proud" of *others*—of our children's scholastic application, for example, or for something fine that someone has accomplished. Saint Paul himself shows his pride in his disciples (2 Cor 1:14, 8:24).

40.   Prudence

Prudence is the first cardinal moral virtue, and consists in the discernment of what is good and what is evil, in order to pursue the one and flee the other, as we conform our aspirations and our activity to the truth.

> "What I am doing is sending you out like sheep among wolves. You must be clever as snakes and innocent as doves" (Mt 10:16). The tendency of the flesh is toward death but that of the spirit toward life and peace (Rm 8:6). Keep careful watch over your conduct. Do not act like fools, but like thoughtful men. Make the most of the present opportunity, for these are evil days (Ep 5:15-16). Scripture says, "I will destroy the wisdom of the wise, and

thwart the cleverness of the clever'' (1 Cor 1:19). It is in Christ and through his blood that we have been redeemed and our sins forgiven, so immeasurably generous is God's favor to us. God has given us the wisdom to understand fully the mystery, the plan he has pleased to decree in Christ . . . (Ep 1:7-10).

Prudence is the source and foundation of all the moral virtues, including the remaining cardinal ones; justice, fortitude, and temperance.

In order to be prudent in the sense of the virtue, we must know the facts, know reality. Otherwise we can neither know the truth nor conform our activity to it, as the definition of prudence requires. So-called "good will" does not suffice.

Do we acquaint ourselves with the facts? Are we not guilty of rash judgment concerning persons and things, as if we were absolutely and vehemently certain of our impressions about them? Have we seriously studied the complex ins and outs of what actually happened, before coming out with our casual, superficial opinions—that is, our imprudent opinions?

In order to be prudent in the sense of the virtue, we must become interested in *how to arrive* at a morally good outcome. That is, we have to be interested in the means, the pathways, to the attainment of the objectives which our intellect has proposed to us as true and good. We may not use evil means to achieve a good end.

Do we not abuse our liberty by availing ourselves of any and every means to achieve the end we have proposed ourselves? Do we not pervert our natural tendency to good by using immoral means. Do we believe the false maxim, "The end justifies the means"?

It is imprudent of one not to take counsel and deliberate concerning the end which one desires to achieve. It is very important to avoid haste—to take the necessary time to engage in mature deliberation.

Are we so impatient and immature that we would like to "skip" this important step in the prudential process? Do we believe that our own opinion suffices for the formation of a judgment and a consequent move to action? Do we set ourselves our supernatural end as our ultimate goal in all things?

It is imprudent not to be constant and persevering. At times, the deliberation we need seems to be taking so long that we stop deliberating! Then how can we go into action? The good end to be attained is vitiated in its very beginnings.

Are we persevering in our good purposes, knowing that constancy will engender sure, firm steps for action (Rm 5:4)?

It is imprudent to have a "bad memory." That is, it is against the virtue of prudence not to submit to the laws of the truth that are a reality. We might put it this way: We are being imprudent if we fail to allow reality be the criterion and measure of our acts, and move instead in categories of "I guess" and "It seems to me as."

Is this the sort of imprudent persons we are? Or do we "read" reality, in order to obey it? Do I take people, and life, *as they are*—or as I should like them to be?

It is imprudent to be lacking in "docility." Docility, in its proper sense, is the attitude of one who rejects the undisciplined mentality of always having to be in the right. He or she is "docile" who accepts the advice of the wise and prudent.

Do we have docility like this? We are not suggesting that one should be passive. Are we humble enough to search out, ask, and accept counsel?

It is imprudent not to have the virtue of "sagacity," which means the ability to remain objective in the face of unexpected difficulties, and to be assiduous in overcoming them. Accordingly, the prudent person will be capable of "tapping the rudder" once in a while—flexible enough to change course a bit when reality so ordains.

Are we inflexible? Or are we too stubborn to take an unexpected turn once we have determined upon a course?

It is imprudent not to have the foresight to be really certain that the means chosen will actually lead to the desired end. Have not a great many of our projects failed owing to imprudence? Have we been overconfident, and dispensed ourselves from exercising the caution we should have had?

It is imprudent not to be cautious and circumspect in making decisions—just as it is imprudent to neglect making them.

It is imprudent to substitute a concern with temporal goods for the quest of a human being's true purpose in life. This is the mere ''prudence of the flesh.''

It is imprudent to be ''astute''—that is, handy at deceiving and at not being deceived, so as to be able to concoct all the necessary ruses to attain the end desired. To be ''astute,'' or ''crafty,'' is to be false, selfish, disloyal, intriguing, and cheap. Might we perhaps have to list ourselves in this category of imprudent persons?

It is imprudent to be either rash and temerarious—neglecting to take account of the risks involved—or pusillanimous and faint-hearted— inhibited by indecisiveness and fearfulness. Neither attitude will attain the morally good end we propose ourselves. Am I audacious and temerarious? Am I given to fear and cowardice?

There is no greater prudence than to choose God, the Highest Good, as one's end, and to strive toward him using the means which he himself offers us. As Josef Pieper says: Supernatural prudence can have no other meaning than this: to permit the truth of the being of God and of the world, most profoundly experienced, to be converted into the rule and measure of my own seeking and acting. There can never be any other norm for the human being to follow than being and its truth (for it is in truth that being is made manifest); and there can never be a higher standard for a human being than the absolute being that is God and his truth.

41. Purity

Purity is moderation with regard to the sexual instinct and sensuality, by means of the spiritual influence of an order dictated by reason.

''Rather, put on the Lord Jesus Christ and make no provision for the desires of the flesh (Rm 13:14). Since we live by the spirit, let us follow the spirit's lead (Gal 5:25). My point is that you should live in accord with the spirit and you will not yield to the cravings of the flesh. The flesh lusts against the spirit and the spirit against the flesh; the two are directly opposed. This is why you do not do what your will intends (Gal 5:16-17). Do you not see that your bodies are members of Christ? . . . Shun lewd conduct. Every other sin a man commits is outside his body, but the fornicator sins against his own body. You must know that your body is a temple of the Holy Spirit, who is within—the Spirit you have received from God. You are not your own (1 Cor 6:15, 18-19). "Blest are the single-hearted for they shall see God. (Mt 5:8). What I say to you is: anyone who looks lustfully at a woman has already committed adultery with her in his thoughts (Mt 5:28).

The Apostle Paul gives us several reasons for being pure: (1) Our bodies belong to our Lord (1 Cor 6:13). (2) We are members of Christ (6:15). (3) We are temples of the Holy Spirit (3:16, 6:19). (4) We have been purchased at the price of Christ's Blood (6:20). Impurity prevents us from entering into communion with the Father. Have we ever considered these revealed truths?

The body ought to be subject to the Spirit (1 Cor 9:27, 2 Cor 4:10-11, Gal 5:24, Col 3:5). In order to attain to this condition, we are required to practice temperance (Ep 5:18), the mortification of the senses (1 Cor 9:27), and prudence and purity in our words (Ep 4:29, 5:3-4).

We are asked not to live in accord with the flesh (Rm 8:7-9), but with sobriety and self-control (1 Th 5:1-11; 1 P 1:13, 5:8), in order not to cloud our minds or harden our hearts (Heb 3:12-13; Rm 1:24-27).

Fornication, which is defined as carnal intercourse outside marriage, is expressly condemned in Scripture as contrary to the natural law, as well as to the new law of the children of God (Gal 5:1-9; Col 3:5-8; Ep 5:3-7, 2; Tm 3:5-6; 2 P 2:10-19).

Have we fallen into the sin of fornication, thereby not only doing injury to ourselves, but causing the other party to fall as well, when I have the vocation and responsibility to sanctify that other person instead? Have we committed fornication?

Have we practiced *incest*, which consists in carnal relations between relatives within the degrees covered by the impediments to marriage? Do we realize how serious a sin this is (1 Cor 5:1-2, 2 Cor 2:5-8)?

Have we ever fallen into the sin of *sodomy*, or homosexual acts? If we suffer from a profound inclination toward this act, so that we are moved toward it against our will, have we sought professional help, in order to understand the problem, so that our purpose of amendment may be efficacious (Rm 1:26-27)?

Do we successfully resist the temptation to *masturbation*, which is the act of seeking solitary sexual gratification? Do we realize the selfishness implied in this unshared gratification? Have we made use of the natural and supernatural means to escape this narcissistic quest of self, which is contrary to the will of our Lord and to the laws of nature? Do we endeavor to have a right conscience in this matter, in spite of the assaults of the world, which, instead of laying its poverty before the mercy of God, seeks to have us believe that misery is not misery?

Have we forgotten that other persons are the sons and daughters of God too, and ought to be respected as such? Have we reduced them to mere objects of pleasure, exciting the most primitive instincts of the flesh, thus ignoring both the example of our Lord and human reason, for which we ought to have a profound respect.

42. Repentance

Repentance is contrition and sorrow for having committed some evil, or for not having done the good that could have and should have been done.

> A woman known in the town to be a sinner learned that he was dining in the Pharisee's home. She brought in a vase of perfumed oil and stood behind him at his feet, weeping so that her tears fell upon his feet. Then she wiped them with her hair, kissing them and perfuming them with the oil (Lk 7:37-38). " 'I will break away and return to my father, and say to him, Father, I have sinned against God and against you; I no longer deserve to be called your son' " (Lk 15:18-19).

Are we afflicted with sorrow when we have done something wrong? Or have we become accustomed to feel indifferent about our sinful actions?

Are we afflicted at not being perfect as our heavenly Father is perfect? Or do we neglect a great many good deeds that we could do for others, and which we would have others do for us?

If someone has offended us, and repents of the offense, do we value his or her contrition and sorrow, or do we remain hardened in the face of this expression of conversion?

In view of so many plans that God has for our lives, have we made an effort of efficacious, mature, and carefully considered repentance, in the light of God's Word that lights up these same lives? Or do we refuse repentance, perhaps even refusing to believe in God, in spite of his plans for our joy and salvation (Mt 21:32)?

The Lord God invites us in a fatherly way, through the words of one of the Apostles, to repent our evil thoughts and deeds (Ac 8:22). He invites us to an efficacious repentance—one which will lead to our conversion. Do we realize that this will wipe away all our sins (Ac 3:19)?

Let us not forget the words of the Psalmist: "My sacrifice, O God, is a contrite spirit; a heart contrite and humbled, O God, you will not spurn" (Ps 51:19).

43. Respect of Persons

Respect of persons is favoritism shown to some persons rather than to others for subjective reasons or because of personal feelings—without any regard for merit or right reason, but based on unimportant differences. Practically always, its roots lie in an antipathy or indifference toward others.

> My brothers, your faith in our glorious Lord Jesus Chist must not allow of favoritism. . . . You are acting rightly, however, if you fulfill the law of the kingdom. Scripture has it, "You shall love your neighbor as yourself." But if you show favoritism, you commit sin and are convicted by the law as transgressors (Jm 2:1, 8-9). In prayer you call upon a Father who judges each one justly on the basis of his actions. Since this is so, conduct yourselves reverently during your sojourn in a strange land (1 P 1:17).

A Christian, following in the footsteps of our Lord, is no "respecter of persons"—that is, does not show favoritism, but regards rich and poor, educated and ignorant, with the same eyes (Gal 3:22-28; Ep 6:9).

What of ourselves? Do we not frequently look down on our brother or sister, and decide "not to choose this one"—thus making ourselves guilty of respect of persons (Rm 14:10)?

Do we not tend to determine our relationships by how we "get along" with others, or other shallow considerations, instead of plumbing the depths of the other persons?

The sin of favoritism or respect of persons, is contrary to justice and charity, in as much as it wounds the unity that should reign among Christians.

44. Revenge

Revenge is satisfaction taken for an offense or injury a manner of violent response to a supposed or actual evil sustained.

"You have heard the commandment, 'An eye for an eye, a tooth for a tooth.' But what I say to you is: offer no resistance to injury. When a person strikes you on the right cheek, turn and offer him the other. If anyone wants to go to law over your shirt, hand him your coat as well. . . . My command to you is: love your enemies, pray for your persecutors" (Mt 5:38-40, 44). Never repay injury with injury. . . . If possible, live peaceably with everyone. Beloved, do not avenge yourselves; leave that to God's wrath, for it is written: "Vengeance is mine; I will repay," says the Lord. . . . Do not be conquered by evil but conquer evil with good (Rm 12:17, 19, 21). We know who said, "Vengeance is mine; I will repay," and "The Lord will judge his people" (Heb 10:30).

Unbridled, blind wrath, as well as faults against temperance, can move a human being to vengeance, or revenge which is a distorted, perverted way of "reestablishing justice" by "paying the other person back."

Do we keep our anger within limits? Do we foster a desire for revenge in ourselves by actually looking for reasons that will inflame our violent temper? Is not this desire frequently linked to envy? Am I so lacking in humility that offenses wound me to excess, and arouse vengeful impulses within me?

The final judgment on persons belongs to God. Sooner or later he will do justice, and his verdict will fall on the good and on the evil.

Are we patient in our faith and hope in this justice? Or instead, do we think ourselves so just that our revenge will not be a greater injustice than the one we have suffered? What has become of the New Law of love and forgiveness, which asks us to practice charity toward our enemies? Are we oblivious of the fact that revenge demeans and injures the perpetrator more than it does the victim, since it diminishes his or her very humanity, converting him or her into a slave of passions and impulses?

If we have ever fallen into the sin of revenge, have we asked forgiveness of God and of our brothers and sisters and made restitution for any actual harm we may have done?

45. Selfishness

Selfishness is an immoderate, excessive love of self, resulting in an inordinate attachment to one's own interest at the expense of that of others.

> Do not forget this: there will be terrible times in the last days. Men will be lovers of self . . . (2 Tm 3:1-2). "I have always pointed out to you that it is by such hard work that you must help the weak. You need to recall the words of the Lord Jesus himself, who said, 'There is more happiness in giving than receiving' " (Ac 20:35). "Give to the man who begs from you. Do not turn your back on the borrower" (Mt 5:42). Is it possible that he who did not spare his own Son but handed him over for the sake of us all will not grant us all things besides (Rm 8:32)?

Only by forgetting ourselves shall we become able to discover and encounter the other.

But our disordered passions, our own interests, a lack of a sense of the common good, a lack of respect and esteem for others, continue to concentrate us on ourselves, and so we close our eyes to our brother and sister.

Are we blind to others? Do we want everything for ourselves? Do we seek to be the center of things, and permanent beneficiaries of things which ought to be for the good of all?

One of the means of combating selfishness is almsgiving. But this means will be effective only if what we give does not consist of things we ought to have thrown on the trash heap long ago. Nor is it remarkably unselfish to give away things or money from what we possess in superfluity. This means will be effective only if what we give to charity is taken from what we actually need and have a right to, but are willing to share out of consideration for the needs and rights of others.

Service to my brother and sister (1 P 4:10) will restrain my selfish desire to have my brother and sister look to me and serve me instead. Bearing my neighbor's burdens (Gal 6:2) will make me forget my own, and help me refrain from imposing my demands on others. The practice of hospitality (Rm 13:13; 1 Tm 5:9-10; Heb 13:2) will diminish my inordinate desire for hospitality from others. Keeping in mind my neighbors and their needs (Jm 2:16-17; 1 Jn 3:17) will help me soften my selfish heart and put order in my appetites, placing them in their proper perspective among so many needs of the common good.

Selfishness is "ego-tism." It is a fault against justice and charity because it always puts *me* ahead of others. I inordinately desire to be held more in account than others, and to occupy the central place in everyone's consideration—to be the crystal sun about which all my satellites revolve.

What model of altruism, unselfishness, does Jesus propose to me instead?

46. Service

Service is an attitude of eagerness to please and serve others— willingly, carefully, attentively, and respectfully.

"Anyone among you who aspires to greatness must serve the rest, and whoever wants to rank first among you must serve the needs of all" (Mt 20:26-27). "If anyone would serve me, let him follow me; where I am, there will my servant be. If anyone serves me, him the Father will honor" (Jn 12:26). "Who, in fact, is the greater—he who reclines at table or he who serves the meal? Is it not the one who reclines at table? Yet I am in your midst as the one who serves you" (Lk 22:27). Slaves, obey your human masters with the reverence, the awe, and the sincerity you owe to Christ. Do not render service for appearance only and to please men, but do God's will with your whole heart as slaves of Christ. Give your service willingly, doing it for the Lord rather than men (Ep 6:5-7)).

In the New Testament it is the servant who bears witness to the apostolate, worship, and ministry of the Church. It is the one who serves who adores, praises, glorifies, and honors the Servant Christ.

In order to follow Jesus Christ, a constant attitude of service is required (Lk 22:25-26; Mk 10:45; Jn 13:12-16; 2 Cor 4:5; 1 P 5:3)—the excercise of charity as manifested in works (1 Tm 6:17-19; 1 Jn 3:18)—in the consciousness that the Church is at the service of all men and women (Lk 22:19-20). Do we serve *with* charity and *out of* charity?

Faced with disciples whose prideful ambition to "be somebody," Jesus, by word and example, reveals to us that nothing is higher or greater than to be of service to one's brothers and sisters (Mt 20:25-28, 23:8-11; Jn 13:12-17). Are we *proud* of our ability to serve others? This would be contrary to humility. Do we labor intensely out of vainglory or ambition, or out of a spirit of imitation of the Servant Christ?

The absence of a spirit of service betrays our selfishness, our lack of fervor, our individualistic isolation, our indolence and sloth, and our lack of initiative and responsibility.

Are we guilty? In view of the needs of the world and of the Church, in view of the miseries of humanity today, have we offered our service to institutions of social service, or charity, or Church groups? Can our parish or Christian community count on our active, serving presence? Do we cooperate in the missions in some way, or in the work of catechetics, or in another evangelizing endeavor where our services are required? Do we imitate our Lord, who came not to be served but to serve?

Servility is the vice of bad servants. It is blind, base submission to the authority of another (1 Cor 7:23, Jm 2:5-7). Nearly always, servility goes hand in hand with flattery and hypocrisy, which both are forms of lying (Mt 22:16, 28:11-15; Lk 23:8-12; Ep 6:6; Ph 2:12; Col 3:22).

Do we lavish praise on people in authority with the expectation of "getting something" for it? Do we seek to obtain particular benefits, or do we seek the common good and the triumph of truth? Do we realize that the only way to combat servility is to serve with love and truth, and without "respect of persons"—to serve all men and women, especially those who have no way to repay us?

47. Sloth

Sloth is the vice of failing to do our work, the vice of wasting time.

> Our desire is that each of you show the same zeal till the end, fully assured of that for which you hope. Do not grow lazy, but imitate those who, through faith and patience, are inheriting the promises (Heb 6:11-12). Refuse to enroll the younger widows . . . they learn to be ladies of leisure, who go about from house to house—becoming not only time-wasters, but gossips and busybodies as well, talking about things they ought not (1 Tm 5:11, 13). Indeed, when we were with you we used to lay down the rule that anyone who would not work should not eat (2 Th 3:10).

Saint Paul warns his contemporaries very bluntly, "Anyone who would not work should not eat," in order to emphasize the injustice of sloth.

Are we lazy and slothful? Do we rise late in the morning, thereby wasting time which will never return? Do we live like ladies and gentlemen of leisure, with all the time in the world on our hands, never lifting a finger to support those with whom we live (Ac 20:33-35; 1 Cor 9:4-18)? The highest motives for not living a life of sloth are the hope of an eternal reward (2 P 1:10-11) and the imitation of our Lord Jesus Christ (Mt 13:53; Mk 6:3).

But there are other reasons, too. We have an obligation to work because we are citizens (1 Cor 9:6), to earn a respectable living (1 Th 2:9).

To be out of work and wandering the streets is a great evil for society, as well as for the individual.

Have the talents we have received borne fruit (Mt 25:15-28), or have we buried them in the earth where they have produced nothing? Have we sadly wasted time? Does too much leisure lead us to devote our time to activities unworthy of a Christian? Are we among those who "kill time" instead of, shall we say "making time come alive"?

Have we resented it when our elders have reproached us for our sloth? At work, do we indulge in sloth and laziness, so that we fail to discharge our duties properly? Have we exerted an *effort* to gain the Kingdom—do we "work for it"?

48. Suffering

Suffering is any painful, adverse reality requiring patience and resignation in the face of physical or moral injury.

In reply Jesus said: "What an unbelieving and perverse lot you are! . . . How long can I endure you?" (Mt 17:17). "I have a baptism to receive. What anguish I feel till it is over!" (Lk 12:50). When Jesus saw her weeping . . . he was troubled in spirit, moved by the deepest emotions. . . . Jesus began to weep (Jn 11:33, 35). He took along Peter and Zebedee's two sons, and began to experience sorrow and distress. Then he said to them, "My heart is nearly broken with sorrow. . . ." In his anguish he prayed with all the greater intensity, and his sweat became like drops of blood falling to the ground (Mt 26:37; Lk 22:44). My brothers, count it pure joy when you are involved in every sort of trial. Realize that when your faith is tested this makes for endurance. . . . Happy the man who holds out to the end through trial! Once he has been proved, he will receive the crown of life the Lord has promised to those who love him (Jm 1:2-3, 12).

The life of Christ is a life marked by suffering. He is born poor (Lk 2:6-7). His parents have to flee to Egypt to escape Herod's persecution (Mt 2:13-15).

He is ill-treated (Lk 4:16-30). He is accounted a mad person, or possessed by the devil (Mk 3:20-21). He has nowhere to lay his head (Mt 8:20).

People reject his gift of love (Jn 6:60-66). He foresees the Passion he will have to suffer (Lk 9:21-22, 44-45, 18:31-34). He suffers from his disciples' lack of faith (Mk 9:18).

He is saddened by the hardness of people's hearts in Jerusalem (Lk 13:34-35). He weeps at the death of his friend Lazarus (Jn 11:33-35).

He sweats blood in his agony in the Garden of Gethsemane (Lk 22:44). He is arrested and put on trial (Mk 14:43-64). He hears Peter's triple denial (Jn 18:18-27). He is struck (Lk 23:63-65). He is subjected to ridicule and contempt (Lk 23:11). He suffers the unjust verdict of the priests, Pilate, and the people (Mk 15:1-13). He is scourged and crowned with thorns, struck and spat upon (Mk 15:15-19). He is stripped of his clothing (Mk 15:20). He suffers abandonment and death (Mt 27:32-56).

Are we deeply affected by the sight of this "Man of Sorrows," considering that he suffers for our sins and for our salvation?

Not all suffering is meritorious. Pain often leads to despair. But the Christian ought to suffer in a Christian manner—with joy and hope (Jm 1:2-4), knowing that everything comes from God's hand (Jm 1:5-12). Is this how we suffer? Do we suffer with fortitude and hope, or with the discouragement of the utterly defeated?

Do we believe, in the midst of our suffering, in God's love? Do we know that, even if he sometimes permits it for a greater good, evil never comes from God himself (Jm 1:13-18)? Do we know that there is no Christian life without the cross, and that without it we are not worthy of Christ (Mt 10:38, 16:34)?

Do we realize that we ought to join our sufferings to those of Jesus, in order that they may be redemptive and lead to Life?

Is suffering a force for salvation for me as a Christian? Or am I
scandalized by it (1 Cor 1:10-24)?

Salvation comes only by blood (Col 1:20). Only the sight of the blood
of the suffering Christ will keep us from falling into despair (Heb 12:2-3)
when faced with physical or mental pain, abandonment, injustice, misun-
derstanding, anguish, loneliness, sickness, and death.

Do we know how to suffer, or do we fall into sadness and loss of faith
when we have to face the cross? Do we deny Jesus' painful, sorrowful
Passion by forgetting that we are to "fill up what is wanting" in that
Passion?

49. Temperance

Temperance is the cardinal moral virtue which moderates the appetites and the use of the senses by cultivating sober discretion, ordering
them in the light of reason.

> Jesus replied, "Scripture has it: 'Not on bread alone is man to live
> but on every utterance that comes from the mouth of God' " (Mt
> 4:4). Those who belong to Christ Jesus have crucified their flesh
> with its passions and desires (Gal 5:24). What I do is discipline my
> own body and master it for fear that after having preached to others
> I myself should be rejected (1 Cor 9:27). Therefore let us not be
> asleep like the rest but awake and sober! (1 Th 5:6). As obedient
> sons, do not yield to the desires that once shaped you in your
> ignorance (1 P 1:14). Stay sober and alert. Your opponent the devil
> is prowling like a roaring lion looking for someone to devour (1 P
> 5:8).

"Temperance," in common usage, has had its meaning reduced to
"moderation in food and drink"—especially in the quantity of food and
drink. By not eating and drinking much we are practicing "temperance"
in the common acceptance of the term. What is emphasized is the
negative aspect of restraint and limitation.

Are we "temperate," even in this popular, incomplete meaning of
the word?

St. Thomas Aquinas says that the first and most immediate effect of
temperance is "tranquility of spirit"—not, however, implying any passivity or static condition. Let us not forget that the purpose of temperance

is to establish order in a human being's heart and mind. This means that my "I" must perform a great deal of activity.

Temperance enables us to preserve our "I" and augment its riches in an unselfish way. This virtue takes the form of shape of other virtues "under" it, such as chastity, sobriety, humility, "meekness" (or gentleness), and seriousness or earnestness. The opposed vices—the forms of *in*temperance—are, respectively, sensuality, lack of self control, pride, unreasonable anger, and idle curiosity.

Do we habitually practice these virtues and resist these vices?

Does *chastity* have real meaning for us? Chastity is that great virtue which, as Joseph Pieper says, "moderates the sexual instinct by means of the spiritual influence of an order dictated by reason." Do we realize what self-destruction the vice of sensuality, or unchastity, leads to? Or do we fall into the opposite trap, and become over-scrupulous about chastity, as if sexuality were something evil? On the contrary, St. Thomas Aquinas tells us clearly that to yield to the natural appetite arising from the sexual instinct and to enjoy the pleasure it brings is a "preeminent good," provided this be done in accord with right order and appropriate means.

Do we really grasp with our intelligence that acts against chastity are not only subjectively sinful by reason of the disorder they entail within the individual, but that, principally, they are offenses against justice, whose object is the common good?

Are we serious about that exercise of temperance which consists in *fasting*, or other forms of asceticism or *mortification of the senses* (Rm 6:12, 8:12-13; 2 Cor 4:16-18, 8:2-5)? Do we look upon fasting as a mere "religious custom," relegated almost entirely to Holy Week? Or do we see it as something based on nature, something useful for bringing the disorders of our sensuality under the domination of reason, so as to be able to appreciate the values of the spirit?

Have I profited by special liturgical times and seasons, Lent, for exmple, for this type of spiritual exercise, either alone or with my family? Do I order my self-denial in a social direction by seeing to it that someone else profits from what I save by my occasional fasts or other sacrifices (2 Cor 8:2-5)?

Have we allowed ourselves to be overcome by *gluttony* (Rm 13:13-

14; 1 Cor 11:17-21)? Do we not realize that everything we do, even eating, ought to be in order to please the Lord and render him glory (Rm 14:6; 1 Cor 10:31), as well as to edify our neighbor (1 Cor 10:23-24, 33), following the example of Jesus (Rm 15:3)?

Do we fully appreciate that gluttony is a form of idolatry (Ph 3:10), since we take a means and make it an end?

Seriousness, or earnestness, is opposed to *curiosity*, in as much as this virtue and vice are, respectively, "temperance, (and the absence of temperance), in pleasure, which proportions and shapes the sensory perception of the cognitive wealth the world has to offer" (Pieper).

Do we lack a sense of due proportion, order, and measure? Do we have the "curious itch," which makes people devotees of the superficial and dilettantes of "snobism"? Or on the contrary, do we love seriousness, and attentive study, in order really to learn the truth of things? We should be lovers of all truth, of course, for all truth flows from and images the Supreme Truth which is God. Do we have frequent recourse to Sacred Scripture, which provides such a compendious access to truth? Or instead, do we sadly waste our time in the pursuit of whatever excites our curiosity, and so forfeit the pleasure of seeking and finding truth?

Let us not forget that humility and gentleness, together with that greatness and loftiness of spirit called "magnaminity," or "greatheartedness," are virtues we have to practice to keep our temperance from being either Manichaean or Pharisaical. (The Manichees, in the time of St. Augustine, held that, as spirit was intrinsically good, so matter was intrinsically evil, and could not be made good. Thus all physical pleasure, for example, was necessarily evil.)

Do we have the virtue of maganimity? Do we love great things in a great way, ordering our "temperate" will of God and the good?

50. Temptation

Temptation is an impulse or enticement to the perpetration of something evil.

"Subject us not to the trial but deliver us from the evil one" (Mt 6:13). "Be on guard, and pray that you may not undergo the test. The spirit is willing but nature is weak" (Mt 26:41) No test has been sent you that does not come to all men. Besides, God keeps his promise. He will not let you be tested beyond your strength. Along with the test he will give you a way out of it so that you may be able to endure it (1 Cor 10:13). Happy the man who holds out to the end through trial! Once he has been proved, he will receive the crown of life. . . . No one who is tempted is free to say, "I am being tempted by God." Surely God, who is beyond the grasp of evil, tempts no one. Rather, the tug and lure of his own passion tempts every man (Jm 1:12-14). Since he was himself tested through what he suffered, he is able to help those who are tempted (Heb 2:18).

In the Lord's Prayer, when we ask God not to lead us into temptation, we are not really asking him to see to it that we have no temptations at all; rather, we are asking him for the strength to resist the temptations which in his providence he allows to come upon us in order to attain a greater good.

Frequently the faithful whose conscience is not very well "formed" accuse themselves in confession of having "had temptations which I resisted." Thus they are accusing themselves of good action—resisting temptation!

Have we been faithful to God's grace, and struggled to resist the onslaughts of the "evil one"?

Christ himself was tempted, in the desert (Mt 4:8-11), and emerged victorious over the Devil. Do we imitate Him? Do we answer, with Jesus, "Not on bread alone is man to live," "You shall not put the Lord your God to the test," and "You shall do homage to the Lord your God; him alone shall you adore"?

Have we been *watchful and vigilant, and persevering in prayer*, in order to resist the enticements of the old self to sin?

Have we committed *presumption* in time of temptation, thinking we could resist it without God's help? Have we committed *despair* in temptation, as if God's strength would not be enough in our weakness, despairing of God's forgiveness and mercy, and believing the Lord could permit us to be tempted beyond our strength? Worse still, have we believed that God himself actually sends temptations (Jm 1:13)?

Have not we ourselves frequently been the occasion of our own temptation with our imprudence, by "playing with fire"? If so, we cannot exonerate ourselves from any unhappy results of this temptation (1 Jm 1:14).

51. Theft

Theft is any action by which one takes another's property for oneself.

"You know the commandments: 'You shall not kill; You shall not commit adultery; You shall not steal; You shall not bear false witness; You shall not defraud; Honor your father and your mother' " (Mk 10:19). "Wicked designs come from the deep recesses of the heart . . . thefts, murder . . . "(Mk 7:21). Can you not realize that the unholy will not fall heir to the kindgdom of God? . . . No . . . thieves . . . will inherit God's kindgom (1 Cor 6:9-10). The man who has been stealing must steal no longer; rather, let him work with his hands at honest labor so that he will have something to share with those in need (Ep 4:28). See to it that none of you suffers for being a murderer, a thief . . . (1 P 4:15).

Theft is a violation of the Seventh Commandment of the Law of God: "You shall not steal" (Ex 20:15).

The Word of God speaks to us on various occasions of the evil of stealing and of the justice which thieves will have to face before the judgment seat of God (Mt 15:19-20; 1 Cor 6:9-10; Ep 4:28).

Let us not think that a thief is necessarily a person who robs an abandoned house, or a pickpocket, or a "mugger." No, many a thief fails to appear in the police blotter in the newspapers.

What about someone who overcharges for his or her goods or services? Is he or she not taking from another what belongs to that other? Is he or she not taking and keeping what is not his or her own?

What about someone who fails to pay a just wage? Is he or she not keeping what belongs to someone else? And if I do not pay my debts—am I not making a profit on goods not my own? After all, this is what "theft" is, by definition.

What about cheating at games of chance where money is involved? Is that not a form of theft, of stealing—an unjust fashion of taking and keeping what rightfully belongs to another, who should have been the one to win it?

Stealing is a violation of justice, and hence entails an obligation of restitution.

Rarely do we realize the importance of "little thefts"—small amounts of money a child may take without the knowledge of his or her parents for example or pocketing the change even though one knows the vendor made a mistake and gave back too much. The reason this can seem of little importance is that it may cause little or no actual injury to the victim in such a small matter. But just as one who is faithful to the Lord in small matters will be faithful to him in larger ones, so a small act of infidelity will dispose us to graver faults.

Do we appreciate attitudes like this, or do we think all this to be unimportant?

52.   Unity

Unity is oneness or agreement among human beings.

"I am in the world no more, but these are in the world as I come to you. O Father most holy, protect them with your name which you have given me that they may be one, even as we are one . . . that all may be one as you, Father, are in me, and I in you; I pray that they may be one in us, that the world may believe that you sent me. I have given them the glory you gave me that they may be one, as we are one—I living in them, you living in me—that their unity may be complete. So shall the world know that you sent me, and that you loved them as you loved me" (Jn 17:11, 21-23). "I have other sheep that do not belong to this fold. I must lead them, too, and they shall hear my voice. There shall be one flock then, one shepherd" (Jn 10:16). God is faithful, and it was he who called you to fellowship with his Son, Jesus Chist our Lord (1 Cor 1:9). All of us have been given to drink of the one Spirit (1 Cor 12:13). What we have seen and heard we proclaim in turn to you so that you may share life with us. This fellowship of ours is with the Father and with his Son, Jesus Christ (1 Jn 1:3). Make every effort to preserve the unity which has the Spirit as its origin and peace as its binding force. . . . Till we become one in faith and in the knowledge of God's Son, and form that perfect man who is Christ come to full stature (Ep 4:3, 13). The grace of the Lord Jesus Christ, and the love of God, and the fellowship of the Holy Spirit be with you all! (2 Cor 13:13).

Christian unity is communion in faith and charity in the bosom of the One Church, which is unified by the work of the Holy Spirit.

A unity of brothers and sisters is a most excellent fruit of the work of Christ. Consequently, disunion is a grave sin. It dismembers the Mystical Body of our Lord.

Have I been a good son or daughter of God in the Church, and a good brother or sister to my brothers and sisters? Or have I been the occasion of division and discord? Do I seek what unifies, or am I inclined to discover and publicize elements which separate us?

Have I fostered unity by fostering my faith—rejecting all heresy, schism, or opinion contrary to the magisterium of the Church, as well as all unfounded criticism? Have I taken into account that charity builds and unites, while cunning, loveless criticism foments dissension?

Have I sought to toil in common with others, persons of good faith? Or has my immaculate, exalted individualism separated me from others?

Do I consider that disunion among Christians is a scandal in the Church that must be overcome? Or have I accepted this state of things? Do I pray for those who bear the name of Christian, that we may all quickly become one flock under one shepherd? Am I superficial in my desires for union, failing to reckon with the gravity of the problems to be resolved? Or on the contrary, am I so rigid in my so-called "orthodox" attitudes that I actually look with criticism and disfavor on the ecumenical work of the Church?

In my everyday family life, am I concerned for family unity, as well as for the readiness of an "open family" to gather to itself, as a nucleus, all those who seek to grow in and enjoy this communion of brothers and sisters that Christ wished? Or do I close up my promises like a ghetto?

Am I stubborn in my opinions, closing off the avenues to dialogue that are required for unity, and oneness among brothers and sisters?

53. Vocation

A vocation is the inspiration with which God calls human beings to follow him in a state of life suited to their abilities and inclinations, in the imitation of Christ in his merciful healing of actual, concrete human miseries.

"No one can come to me unless the Father who sent me draws him; I will raise him up on the last day" (Jn 6:44). He said to them, "Come after me and I will make you fishers of men." They immediately abandoned their nets and became his followers. He walked along farther and caught sight of two other brothers, James Zebedee's son, and his brother John. They too were in their boat, getting their nets in order with their father, Zebedee. He called them, and immediately they abandoned boat and father to follow him (Mt 4:19-22). As he moved on he saw Levi the son of Alphaeus at this tax collector's post, and said to him, "Follow me." Levi got up and became his follower (Mk 2:14). When Jesus heard this he said to him: "There is one thing further you must do. Sell all you have and give to the poor. You will have treasure in heaven. Then come and follow me" (Lk 18:22-23).

Our great vocation is to be *followers of Christ*, similar to the disciples of Jesus.

But it is important to notice that these disciples, as soon as they heard our Lord's voice, *left everything and followed him at once*. Is this our attitude as well? Do we make an effort to discern our vocation in the world and in the Church? Or on the contrary, have we chosen our profession or state of life out of selfish, cheap, or material considerations? Are we not even concerned about it, so that we do not even bother to think what our true vocation might be?

Are we faithful to Christ's own calling, which was to be obedient to the Father in all things? If our conscience tells us we ought to embrace the religious or priestly state, do we become discouraged by the pressures of the world, or the obstacles our family places in our way? Do we seek to embrace a particular, concrete vocational state out of a spirit of service? Or do we embrace it on account of its supposed dignity, and the recognition it will bring with it? Do we overcome the difficulties that prevent the Lord's call from "getting through" to us?

Do we realize that the Christian vocation to freedom, obedience, and the following of Christ implies a vocation to holiness, and that we are therefore all called to holiness?

Do we think we can achieve this holiness without the cross?

Do we nurture our vocation, our call, or does the voice of Christ fall on deaf ears?

54. Weakness

Weakness is a lack of vigor and energy of spirit, so that we are particularly prone to yeild to opposition or to emotion.

> "Be on guard, and pray that you may not undergo the test. The spirit is willing but nature is weak" (Mt 26:41). Extend a kind welcome to those who are weak in faith. Do not enter into disputes with them (Rm 14:1). God chose those whom the world considers absurd to shame the wise; he singled out the weak of this world to shame the strong (1 Cor 1:27). We exhort you to admonish the unruly; cheer the fainthearted; support the weak; be patient toward all (1 Th 5:14).

Jesus showed a preference for children and weak persons. Our own charity, as well, should be greater in degree toward those who are less able to do things for themselves (Rm 14:1, 15:1; 1 Cor 9:22, 12:22-26). Do we tend to seek out, find, protect, and aid the very weakest?

We have to go back to Jesus' testimony for our example in this matter. *Jesus chose the weak* (Rm 5:6, 6:9; 2 Cor 12:5-9, 13:4-9), in order to show us that it is He who can do all things, and that without Him we can do nothing. Without him, we are weakness.

We ought not to glory too much in our own strength, for we know that, often enough, our intentions have been good, but we have flagged in the struggle (Mt 26:41, Mk 14:38. Are we too confident of ourselves, so that we believe too much in our own abilities? Is this not presumption?

Those who are strong should come to the aid of the weak, and those who are weak should joyfully and humbly lean on the strong (2 Cor 13:9). Are we, instead, a stumbling block for the weak, hindering their growth, and excluding them from our world (1 Cor 9:9) on the implicit pretext of our "freedom of the mighty"?

It is comforting and encouraging to see that Saint Paul was strong when he felt himself to be weak (2 Cor 12:10). He knew that the power of God operated only in his littleness. Do we accept our weakness, our littleness, our limitations, with joy and patience? And when we see the same weakness, littleness, and limitations in our neighbor, does that exasperate us, or does it move us to mercy?

55. Wealth

Wealth is an abundance of possessions and things of value.

> "If you seek perfection, go, sell your possessions, and give to the poor. You will then have treasure in heaven." . . . Hearing these words the young man went away sad, for his possessions were many. Jesus said to his disciples: "I assure you, only with difficulty will a rich man enter into the kingdom of God" (Mt 19:21-23). "How blest are the poor in spirit; the reign of God is theirs (Mt 5:3). Let the brother in humble circumstances take pride in his eminence and the rich man be proud of his lowliness, for he will disappear "like the flower of the field" (Jm 1:9-19). Those who want to be rich are falling into temptation and a trap. They are letting themselves be captured by foolish and harmful desires which drag men down to ruin and destruction. . . . Tell those who are rich in this world's goods not to be proud, and not to rely on so uncertain a thing as wealth. Let them trust in the God who provides us richly with all things for our use. Charge them to do good, to be rich in good works and generous, sharing what they have (1 Tm 6:9, 17-18). I ask you, how can God's love survive in a man who has enough of this world's goods yet closes his heart to his brother when he sees him in need (1 John 3:17).

True riches consist in the knowledge that one's possessions will pass away, and that the only wealth which will not pass away is God and his Kingdom of love.

Christ gives us the example. He was born poor (Lk 2:7, 24). He lived poor (Mt 8:18-22). He suffered hunger and thirst (Mt 21:18, Jn 19:28). He had nowhere to lay his head (Mt 8:20) He died stripped of everything he had (Jn 19:23-42).

And yet he does not cut himself off from the rich. Indeed, we see "good rich people" in Scripture—Nicodemus, Joseph of Arimathea, Lazarus, Zacchaeus (who was converted by Jesus' visit)—and "bad rich people," like the buyers and sellers in the Temple, or the rich person in the parable of Lazarus.

Our Lord does not say it is *impossible* for a rich person to be saved, he says it is *difficult* (Mt 19:23-26). Possessions generate a fondness in us. Consequently it is difficult to detach oneself from them and go out to God and one's brother and sister.

Christ permits the possession of private property, but he insists on their right use (Lk 14:12-14, 16:1-12; Mt 26:9-11). The Apostles have likewise left us their testimony on this point (Ph 4:11-12; 1 Tm 6:7-8; Rv 3:17, 18:9-19; 1 Tm 6:9-10, 17-18).

Do I use my possessions, or do they use me?

Christ wishes us to become involved in the building of a *new* world, *another* world. If I assign money the highest place in my scale of values (1 Tm 6:9-10), am I not falling into the most common of vices, and one that hinders our search for genuine wealth? In the actual reality of the everyday world, is not money the great bone of contention, the great cause of unpleasantness and broken friendship? Is it not the great motive for striking up special-interest "friendships"? Does it not seem that "friendships" among nations are often nothing but "money clubs"?

Is this the new, better world Christ is calling us to build? To which world are we ourselves committed, this one or the new one?

Do we seek to share our possessions with all men and women, especially with those most in need? Do we practice "solidarity" with respect to our wealth, or do we consider it property so "private" that it becomes incommunicable? Do we realize that, while there is indeed a right to private property, this property also has a social function?

As members of a Catholic community, do we contribute, according to our ability, to the *material maintenance* of our parish, its worship, and its works of charity? Do we contribute to the needs of the diocese and the greater Church in these areas? If not, is this because we look down on the Church as something too little for our great selves, so that we either ignore, or consider ourselves exempt from, our obligation in its regard (Gal 6:6; 1 Cor 9:1-14)?

So many people in the world today live in a state of misery—the fruit of our society's economic mismanagement and unwise structures. Is this not a real scandal and injustice? Have we failed to unite our efforts with those of other men and women of good will in order to try to find an in-depth solution to this problem—or at least to mitigate its negative effects?

Do we live soberly as individuals and as families, using our goods and property as they are meant to be used? Or on the contrary, are we ostentatious in our outlay and expenditures, so that our trips, entertainments, home furnishings, food, and drink constitute a real case of squandering? Do we set aside a part of our monthly budget for the alleviation of other people's misery? Do we know that our superfluities *do not belong to us*, and that, quite often, it will be not only a matter of charity, but of justice, to share even our necessary possessions with others?

Do we teach our children—without undue stinginess, but with firmness to have a right appreciation of the value of material goods and money? Do we exhort them to generosity, as well as to a moderate appetite for all the many things a consumer society has to offer them?

Have we learned by experience that it is more blessed to give than to receive (Ac 20:35)?

56. Worldliness

Worldliness is an exaggerated attachment to the things of the world, its frivolities, and its pleasures.

> O you unfaithful ones, are you not aware that love of the world is enmity to God? (Jm 4:4). Have no love for the world, nor the things that the world affords. If anyone loves the world, the Father's love has no place in him. . . . Carnal allurements, enticements for the eye, the life of empty show—all these are from the world (1 Jn 2:15-16). We know that we belong to God, while the whole world is under the evil one (1 Jn 5:19). "I gave them your word, and the world has hated them for it; they do not belong to the world any more than I belong to the world. I do not ask you to take them out of the world, but to guard them from the evil one" (Jn 17:14-15). "I tell you all this that in me you may find peace. You will suffer in the world. But take courage! I have overcome the world" (Jn 16:33).

The world, understood as the universe of creatures, is a work of God, and therefore good (Jn 1:3; Ac 4:24, 14:14, 17:24; Rm 11:36; Heb 1:10, Rv 4:11). We should love all creation as coming from the hand of God.

This world of ours, this universe we live in, is preserved and governed by God, who exercises his merciful Providence over it (Jn 5:17; Heb 1:3; Ph 2:13; Mt 5:45, 6:26, 31-32; 1 Cor 12:6).

Our world, and all that it contains, are for the glory of God (Rm 11:34-36; 1 Cor 15:28, 3:22-23). As I contemplate this fact, do I have an attitude of thanksgiving for this creation bestowed on human beings, and for God's loving providence, his foresight, shown toward his creatures? Do we deal with creation in such a way that it can give glory to God?

But "world" is used in a different sense in Sacred Scripture. Here, the "world" is the kingdom of the "worldly," those who hinder the redeeming work of Christ (Lk 16:8; Jn 1:10, 12:31, 14:17, 27, 15:18, 16:33; 1 Cor 1:27, 2:6, 12, 3:18; Jm 4:4). We are immersed in a "world" that struggles against the Lord. But even though we are immersed in it, we cannot belong to it (Jn 17:14, 16).

Are we "worldly"? That is, are we among those who direct their gaze toward the things of earth, toward this fleeting world (1 Cor 7:31), forgetting that Christ has opened other doors to us, and that these are the doors that lead to our true homeland?

Are we "frivolous," lavishing too much time, concern, and money on our body and our clothes? Do we go through life thinking about what the latest film or TV star has done and trying to be "just like" him or her? Do we follow the rhythm of fashion's dictates, obeying Madison Avenue's every command?

Are we worldly in our words and gestures, lacking in modesty and the "sobriety of the children of God"? Do we allow ourselves to be pulled along by the cry of the herd, without any judgment of our own, or any reasoning on which to base such a judgment? Have we watered down our personhood into a personhood of "the world," a worldly personality, instead of giving it a good dose of "Christian tonic"?

Have we preferred the "things of earth" to the "things above" by choosing badly (Col 3:1-2)?

57. Will of God

The will of God is God's decree, determination, disposition, or permission tending to human beings' fulfillment of their vocation to holiness and the implementation of his plan in their history.

Jesus explained to them: "Doing the will of him who sent me and bringing his work to completion is my food" (Jn 4:34). "It is not to do my own will that I have come down from heaven, but to do the will of him who sent me. It is the will of him who sent me that I should lose nothing of what he has given me; rather, that I should raise it up on the last day" (Jn 6:38-39). "Whoever does the will of God is brother and sister and mother to me" (Mk 3:35). "Your kingdom come, your will be done on earth as it is in heaven" (Mt 6:10). [Paul] answered with a question: "Why are you crying and breaking my heart in this way? For the name of the Lord Jesus I am prepared, not only for imprisonment, but for death, in Jerusalem." Since he would not be dissuaded, we said nothing further except, "The Lord's will be done" (Ac 21:13-14).

The will of God is his glory and our sanctification.

In the Our Father, we pray that the will of God may always be done. Do we act in such a way that this loving desire on our part will actually be effective? Do we restrain our own will, with its capriciousness and fallibility, conforming it to the will of God?

The will of God can never seek our misfortune, although at times it may permit a particular evil in order that we may receive a greater good.

Is this how we interpret life's misfortunes?

Do we forget that our Lord knows what is good for us, truly good, at every moment of our lives, much better than we do ourselves?

Do we call God's judgment and love into question by passing judgment on his will?

In fulfilling God's will, do we take into account that the ties that bind us to him are stronger than any ties of flesh and blood (Lk 8:19-21)?

Do we practice a passive, fatalistic resignation in the face of life's events, saying blandly, "It is the will of God"? Or do we call forth God's will, as it were, by our active availability for the action of grace—by seeking what is true and good?

Do we seek to distinguish between the will of God and the will of human beings in the occurrences of life (Ep 5:17), knowing that in order to gain the Kingdom we must fulfill His will and not our own petty projects?

Chapter 3

Celebration of the Sacrament of Penance

Now that we have examined our conscience according to one of the above forms—not to exclude other ways of reviewing our life in the light of Christ, of course—we come to a consideration of just how to "go to confession."

The reception of this Sacrament, like that of all the others, is called a "celebration." In the other Sacraments the aspect of celebration is more obvious. In the Eucharist especially, we perform actions in concert with a large number of the faithful. The liturgy of confession, however, is very likely to be restricted to an encounter between a confessor and a penitent.

And yet it *is* a liturgical celebration, and should be experienced as such. It is an action of Christ and the Church for communicating God's life to human beings and rendering God his due worship.

Sacramental Penance is an act of human beings' sanctification, as is evident from the fact that forgiveness of our sins is granted there.

It is an act of religion, and an act of faith.

It is an act of prayer, whereby a human being moves toward his or her God and Lord acknowledging Him, giving Him thanks and begging of Him things that will be for our good—the things He has and wishes to share with us. This sacramental action combines all the requirements for true prayer.

True, when confessions are heard during Sunday Mass (a common practice, and not a very ideal one), there is no way to experience the liturgical Rite of Penance as it is presented in the new Ritual. The latter is possible when a smaller number of the faithful assemble, at a scheduled time, for the Sacrament of Reconciliation, and each one can be granted the time his or her situation requires. And when the sacramental action occurs within a community celebration of Penance, then the ecclesial dimension, the Church dimension, of the Sacrament of Reconciliation is reflected and signified best of all. The holy People of God are a sinful people, too, and God bestows his forgiveness on each individual penitent as members of this People, through the ministerial mediation of the Church.

But what would be the ideal way to celebrate this Sacrament in the case of an individual penitent receiving it outside the context of a community Penance service? We shall now proceed with an explanation of such a celebration, step by step, explaining each step separately. For greater clarity, before we explain each step we shall quote exactly what the magisterium of the Church has to say about it in the new Ritual. For it is by reading these texts, living and experiencing the rite according to the steps we shall explain, and penetrating all that the Word of God and the voice of the Church have to say, that we shall be better able to understand what this great Sacrament causes and signifies: we shall be better able to experience this living encounter that occurs between God's proffered pardon, and the need for that pardon now proclaimed by his sinful creature.

A.   The Time of Celebration

13. The reconciliation of penitents may be celebrated at any time on any day, but it is desirable that the faithful know the day and time at which the priest is available for this ministry. They should be encouraged to approach the sacrament of penance at times when Mass is not being celebrated and especially during the scheduled periods.

The season of Lent is most appropriate for celebrating the sacrament of penance.

We have already made a good examination of conscience in the light of the Gospel. Now the moment has come to seek out a confessor.

Ideally, we shall have a regular confessor of our own, someone who knows us interiorly, and can help us, in a familiar way, to be converted to the Lord. But this is not always possible. Hence it is important not to be afraid to approach a priest who is available.

This Sacrament "may be celebrated at any time on any day." All times are good for receiving God's pardon. As an ideal to strive for however—we should not make our confession during the celebration of Holy Mass. If we do, we shall find that neither sacred action will be well celebrated. We shall find ourselves standing in line, "waiting our turn" to go to confession instead of participating in the liturgical action of the Eucharist. Indeed, we shall already have "missed" some part of the Mass by not being able to give it full attention while we were preparing our confession, and hence shall not have been able to participate in it as fully as the authentic notion of liturgy would have us participate. Furthermore, the number of penitents to be heard will generally preclude the use of the complete Rite of Reconciliation; in fact it will be stripped to its bare minimum. Finally, the celebration of the Eucharist, with its readings, singing, and so on, will make it difficult to hear confessions in the confessionals as they are generally located in the church itself. Consequently, so far as possible we should consult the confession schedule for the times when the Sacrament will be celebrated *outside the time of Mass*.

B. Preparation of Priest and Penitent

15.Priest and penitent should first prepare themselves by prayer to celebrate the sacrament. The priest should call upon the Holy Spirit so that he may receive enlightenment and charity. The penitent should compare his life with the example and commandments of Christ and then pray to God for the forgiveness of his sins.

Here the new Ritual is inculcating the importance of preparation. One ought to be suitably disposed for an experience in which two persons, a priest and a penitent enter the relationship of this unique dialogue. They will be experiencing and performing an act of judgment. They will be endeavoring to discern what God thinks of certain things, and what the role of Christ is in this action of free human beings in the exercise of their freedom.

More than one priest, in a spirit of routine professionalism, has perhaps thought of this moment as one in which he awaits a client seeking his services. There is an element of truth in this. But this aspect is purely secondary. What is transpiring here, above and beyond any mere professional-client relationship, is the rendering of a *specifically Christian* service, in which a person-to-person relationship is established

touching delicate nerves of the human psyche and the Christian conscience. The priest will be stepping into an area of the soul reserved to
God alone—where the penitent has freely invited him to come as into a
sanctuary, a Holy of Holies—and there, in the depths of another's soul, to
play his privileged role.

And so one prays. Priest and penitent both beg the Spirit to move
them, with His gifts, to see and to love—move them to discern Christ's
plan, and accordingly to ask and to receive the pardon he has gained for us
by his redeeming Blood.

C.   Welcoming the Penitent

*16.   The priest should welcome the penitent with fraternal charity and,
if the occasion permits, address him with friendly words. The penitent
then makes the sign of the cross, saying:* **In the name of the Father, and
of the Son, and of the Holy Spirit. Amen.** *The priest may also make the
sign of the cross with the penitent. Next the priest briefly urges the
penitent to have confidence in God. If the penitent is unknown to the
priest, it is proper for him to indicate his state in life, the time of his last
confession, his difficulties in leading the Christian life, and anything else
which may help the confessor in exercising his ministry.*

It is most important, as well from the human, psychological point of
view as from that of charity, that the priest receive the penitent with a
brother's love. The penitent is a person. This of itself is a reason for
treating him or her with reverence and consideration. But more than this,
he or she is coming as a *poor* person—a beggar asking for alms. A
penitent is here presenting himself or herself before Christ, just as so
many lepers, blind persons, deaf persons, and paralytics of long ago
made bold to do, begging Him to cleanse them, begging him that they
might see, might hear, might walk. And He received them with human
warmth and Christian love.

The Magisterium of the Church now directs that the penitent be urged
"to have confidence in God." Just as this person has fallen because he or
she has trusted in his or her own strength—that poor, faltering
strength!—so now the path back to God requires a change of focus: he or
she is to lean upon the mighty arm of God. The priest may extend this
invitation in words like these, for example:

**May God, who has enlightened every heart,
help you to know your sins
and trust in his mercy.**
*The penitent answers:***Amen.**

Then the priest may read or say from memory a text of
Scripture which proclaims God's mercy and calls man to conversion.

Among the passages recommended for this (optional) recitation or
reading are: Ez 33:11; Lk 5:32; 1 Jn 2:1-2.

The key ideas of this invitation are the following:

An inner light has led us to this
moment of reconciliation.

It is God who gives me to see my
misery and his great mercy.

It is impossible for God, whom we call
Love, to will our condemnation and
destruction. On the contrary, his will
is for us to live.

We are the field of action of Christ's
mercy. He has come to seek the sheep
that was lost.

Jesus is our Advocate with the Father
for he has given himself as an offering,
in expiation for the sins of the world.

We answer this invitation with a heartfelt "Amen!" We are surely
ready to celebrate this Sacrament of faith.

D. Reading the Word of God

It is not always possible to have a Reading. But we see that the Church
does wish to incorporate the Word of God into the Liturgy of Penance, for
we are making an act of faith, and an act of faith has its causality in God's
Word. Our repentance is not based on human criteria, categories of the
flesh, but on the Divine Word, who has summoned us, and led us to
discover in the light of the Spirit that our conduct has turned down roads
altogether dissimilar from the routes traced out for us by God—routes He
himself revealed when his Word, his Son, spoke to us and begged to
make a response worthy of sons and daughters.

Here is what the Church teaches us about this moment in the sacramental celebration:

17. Then the priest, or the penitent himself, may read a text of holy Scripture, or this may be done as part of the preparation for the sacrament. Through the word of God the Christian receives light to recognize his sins and is called to conversion and to confidence in God's mercy.

The Church offers us a long list of brief biblical passages from which to choose. We cite them here, so that the reader may see just how the Church wishes to lead us in order that we may confront our condition as sinners standing before the Judgment Seat of the Just Judge—who is merciful and loving with his creatures as well.

Isaiah 53:4-6	John 20:19-23
Ezekiel 11:19-20	Romans 5:8-9
Matthew 6:14-15	Ephesians 5:1-2
Mark 1:14-15	Colossians 1:12-14
Luke 6:31-38	Colossians 3:8-10, 12-17
Luke 15:1-7	1 John 1:6-7, 9

In order to personalize the celebration still further, "the priest and penitent may choose other readings from scripture" instead (no. 43).

Now the Word of God, whose mission is illumination, has been sown like good seed in the welcoming earth that is the penitent. And good seed in hospitable ground cannot fail to sprout. We have come to the central moment in the celebration. We have moved ahead another step. We are gradually being penetrated by the mystery of a God who lays himself open to us in pedagogical fashion, in the signs of the Sacraments of the Church.

E.   Confession of Sins and the Act of Penance

This step is clearly set forth in the new Ritual:

18. The penitent then confesses his sins, beginning, where customary, with a form of general confession: I confess to almighty God. *If neces-*

sary, the priest should help the penitent to make a complete confession; he should also encourage him to have sincere sorrow for his sins against God. Finally, the priest should offer suitable counsel to help the penitent begin a new life and, where necessary, instruct him in the duties of the Christian way of life. If the penitent has been the cause of harm or scandal to others, the priest should lead him to resolve that he will make appropriate restitution. Then the priest imposes an act of penance or satisfaction on the penitent; this should serve not only to make up for the past but also to help him to begin a new life and provide him with an antidote to weakness. As far as possible, the penance should correspond to the seriousness and nature of the sins. This act of penance may suitably take the form of prayer, self-denial, and especially service of one's neighbor and works of mercy. These will underline the fact that sin and its forgiveness have a social aspect.

This personal, personalizing moment of the penitent's meeting with Christ in the person of the confessor, is of vital importance. This is the "moment of truth." Now sin has met its match. This is the moment when we seek to have our guilt swept away and the damage we have caused repaired. The moment of confession has arrived.

What are the qualities of a good confession? A good confession must be integral, clear, truthful, and motivated by sincere repentance.

A good confession must be integral. It must include all grave sins committed since our last confession. None may be omitted, either deliberately or by careless forgetfulness.

A good confession must be clear. There must be no disguising of exactly what our sins have been by couching them in too-general terms. The confessor has to know what happened. He is not unwholesomely curious, but after all, it is he who is here as a judge and counsellor, and unless he knows what happened he can neither judge rightly nor give helpful advice and direction. It is true that a wise confessor can often tell what the penitent, especially a child or young person, really has in mind with all the beating about the bush. But it is not always easy, and besides, even young penitents should be taken seriously, and properly trained in the right way to tell their sins. Unclear confessions in childhood will become unclear confessions in adolescence, and the end result will be adults who are incapable of judging themselves.

A good confession must be truthful. We have a Christian duty to know how to make a just appraisal of our moral situation, without putting everything into the wrong categories. Hence attitudes of "scrupulosity" are to be avoided, in which grave sins are seen when there have been only slight ones, or slight ones where there was no sin at all. We must become accustomed to passing an objective judgment on our life.

The opposite error is that of a "lax conscience." Here, one finds neither grave nor slight sins in one's life—simply "mistakes" or "faults," such as everyone has.

The confessor's judgment comes second. *The penitent is his or her own first judge.* Hence the penitent ought not to ask the confessor to assess subjective guilt with questions like, "Was that a sin, Father?" It is true that when there is a genuine ignorance or doubt, the confessional can be the place for counsel or instruction. But more often than not these questions are an evasion of the penitent's responsibility to judge his or her own subjective guilt or innocence.

A good confession must be motivated by sincere repentance, and not by mere human remorse, or by a "bad taste in my mouth" that I have when I have sinned. The main motive for going to confession should be the *knowledge that my conduct has offended God*, has injured my brother or sister, and damaged the holiness of the Church. Everything else is secondary. Confession is not a tranquilizer. Of course, I shall not be surprised if, in fact, I do feel more tranquil when I know I have made my peace with God and have been restored to his friendship.

We cannot expatiate here on all the qualities of a good confession, not even to the extent that we have on the four principal ones. Hence we shall simply list the qualities St. Thomas cites, as he himself has received them from earlier tradition: Confession should be: simple, humble, pure, faithful, frequent, clear, precise, voluntary, without ostentation, integral, secret, sorrowful, prompt, strong, accusing, and obedient. Here we have an excellent check-list for reviewing the quality of our sacramental experience with respect to Penance.

What should be the qualities of the penitential satisfaction—the "penance," that is imposed upon the penitent?

It should be "expiatory," and it should be "medicinal," or remedial. It should restore justice and charity, and it should help the penitent discover the remedy he or she needs to begin a new life. We have already stated in the beginning of this book that the confessor and the penitent should together seek out the right medicines for the latter's particular ailments, and avoid penances that are too general in nature. They should use their ingenuity, in a spirit of charity, to discover expiatory acts, acts of satisfaction, which will really attack the malady, the evil, in its roots.

Let me give an example. A number of years ago, I came across the instance of a woman who, in her sincere repentance for having had an abortion, decided to propose this penance to her confessor: For a period of three years both she and her husband would do volunteer work in a children's hospital. Here was an *effective* way to restore justice. One life had been snuffed out. Now many lives would be cared for, with the love of two people who were indeed "heartily sorry."

F. The Prayer of the Penitent and the Absolution by the Priest

The confession is at an end. The penitent has been oriented in his or her problems and has received adequate advice if necessary. Now let us proceed to the next step in this celebration of God's forgiveness.

19. After this the penitent manifests his contrition and resolution to begin a new life by means of a prayer for God's pardon. It is desirable that this prayer should be based on the words of Scripture.

Liturgy seeks an active participation on the part of the faithful. Hence at this point the new Ritual lists a number of formulae, to be placed by the confessor in the hands of the penitent, expressing the latter's sincere repentance. Any of them may be read or recited by the penitent, or, indeed, one not on the list may be chosen instead. In any case the penitent will now be pronouncing an expression of his or her sincere sorrow for sin. Here are a few of the formulae the Ritual suggests:

> My God,
> I am sorry for my sins with all my heart.
> In choosing to do wrong
> and failing to do good, I have sinned against you
> whom I should love above all things.

I firmly intend, with your help,
to do penance,
to sin no more,
and to avoid whatever leads me to sin.
Our Savior Jesus Christ
suffered and died for us.
In his name, my God, have mercy.

This is surely a beautiful, expressive prayer. In it we can see the following elements:

An affirmation of the penitent's sorrow for actions as well as omissions.

A realization that these offenses have been committed against the most noble of all possible objects: God.

A purpose of amendment, already rightly undertaken. ("With your help.")

A petition for mercy and forgiveness, encouraged by the knowledge that Christ gave his life for his sheep. ("Our Savior Jesus Christ suffered and died for us.")

Here is another formula:

87. Luke 15:18; 18:13
Father, I have sinned against you
and am not worthy to be called your son.
Be merciful to me, a sinner.

The first two lines, from Luke 15, are quoted from our Lord's parable of the Prodigal Son.

The last line, from Luke 18, is what the tax collector said in his prayer to God in our Lord's parable of the Pharisee and the Publican.

Or here is another:

92.
Lord God,
in your goodness have mercy on me:
do not look on my sins,
but take away all my guilt.
Create in me a clean heart
and renew within me an upright spirit.

This is Psalm 51, the "Penitential Psalm" par excellence. In these two verses (11 and 12) we pray to God in the spirit of David—full of repentance and hope, and begging forgiveness.

Then the Ritual goes on with its instructions:

> Following this prayer, the priest extends his hands, or at least the right hand, over the head of the penitent and pronounces the formula of absolution, in which the essential words are: *I absolve you from your sins in the name of the Father, and of the Son, and of the Holy Spirit.*

The priest, the ministerial instrument of Christ in the Church, now crowns the process that began when this Christian believer decided to go and see what Christ thought of him or her. The penitent's brothers and sisters would be consulted, too, on the subject—in the person of their fellow minister of Christ, the priest. Finally, the penitent has had to face what he or she ought to think of his or her own life and conduct. And now the moment has come when Christ Jesus, by the mediation of one of his ministers, pardons and forgives this person who has manifested his or her desire to be so pardoned and forgiven. Extending his hand over the penitent's head—as did our Lord, so many times—the priest says:

> God, the Father of mercies,
> through the death and resurrection of his Son
> has reconciled the world to himself
> and sent the Holy Spirit among us
> for the forgiveness of sins;
> through the ministry of the Church
> may God give you pardon and peace,
> and I absolve you from your sins
> in the name of the Father, and of the Son, †
> and of the Holy Spirit.
> The penitent answers: *Amen.*

And the penitent's sins are forgiven. Pardon has been bestowed, as Christ bestowed it on his contemporaries of Judea and Galilee long ago. Once more the Good Shepherd has made His appearance. For he had discovered that a sheep was missing from the fold—so he went in search of it. He found it and restored it to the fold, and there was great joy in heaven.

This moment, so clearly and carefully emphasized in the celebration, is of supreme importance. Hence the confessor ought to pronounce the formula of absolution in a clear and audible voice, without inserting other formulae (such as the one which begins, "I, a sinner . . ." which is customary in some countries), or any other penitential prayers. These prayers, if used, should be introductory. At this moment it should be the absolution itself, and only the absolution, which is heard, and received in silence by the penitent. It is like a seal, like a signature, on a document, on a treaty of peace between God and a human being—between the Church which has seen its charity grow small in a sinner, and that same sinner, now restored to the bosom of the family like a son or daughter come back to life.

Here is what the Church has to say about the formula of absolution we have just seen:

> As he says the final words the priest makes the sign of the cross over the penitent. The form of absolution (see no. 46) indicates that the reconciliation of the penitent comes from the mercy of the Father; it shows the connection between the reconciliation of the sinner and the paschal mystery of Christ; it stresses the role of the Holy Spirit in the forgiveness of sins; finally, it underlines the ecclesial aspect of the sacrament because reconciliation with God is asked for and given through the ministry of the Church. [19]

Thus we see:

God the Father reconciles the world to himself.

The means He uses for this restoration to His friendship is the Blood of His Son ("Through the death and resurrection of his Son . . .").

It is the Spirit of Pentecost who will make this Paschal Mystery of Christ actually present. For we live in the age of the Spirit, until the Lord returns to judge the living and the dead.

But Christ's Paschal Mystery, made present by the work of the Holy Spirit, has need of the mediation of the Church. Someone who, in the midst of the People of God, holds a special office (that of bishop or priest), will stand as mediator between God and human beings here, and grant the pardon and peace won by the sacrificial offering of Jesus Christ. This is what the Ritual means by "Through the ministry of the Church."

Finally, we note that the absolution is given in the "first person

singular." The priest says, "*I* absolve you." The priest, as duly constituted minister of the Church, has the power of "binding and
loosing"—the power bestowed by our Lord on Peter and the Apostles,
which is passed on to those who receive the two highest degrees of the
Sacrament of Order: the Episcopate and the Priesthood.

The concluding "Amen," which the penitent pronounces in a clear
voice, will be his or her "Yes"—his or her acceptance of the pardon
which the Lord has just bestowed.

Let us repeat, it is important that the penitent hear the absolution
formula in silence—and *in its entirety*, without pronouncing the final
words (". . . in the name of the Father, and of the Son, † and of the Holy
Spirit") along with the priest, as he or she did at the beginning of the
celebration when making the Sign of the Cross.

G. Proclamation of Praise of God and Dismissal

The liturgical celebration of the Sacrament of Penance is at an end.
The penitent has received sacramental absolution, and is about to return
to the street.

The street is a hard place to be. The penitent is returning to daily life,
where the battle of the faith is waged, the bloody struggle that threatens to
destroy us utterly.

But we are returning well armed. We have put on the armor of Christ.
In order to "go and sin no more," we have not so much to rely on the acts
of our own will (although we shall *also* have to have a strong will), but on
a knowledge and love of God, a confidence and trust in his mercy, an
attentive ear to his daily voice, perseverance in prayer, the imitation of
the example of the saints, and their intercession, especially the intercession of Our Lady, Refuge of Sinners.

It will be a matter of opening our minds and hearts, with docility, to
an apprenticeship of the saving Word of God. It will often require
intelligence to carefully discern a sinful situation from a merely emotion-
ally challenging one—between a breakdown in our moral structures and a
mighty onslaught of fear and guilt. We must never confuse the mission of
a confessor with that of a psychiatrist or psychologist, even though many
a situation of modern life will require the intervention of both. For the
Christian is returning to the street. . . .

20. After receiving pardon for his sins the penitent praises the mercy of God and gives him thanks in a short invocation taken from scripture. Then the priest tells him to go in peace. The penitent continues his conversion and expresses it by a life renewed according to the Gospel and more and more steeped in the love of God, for "love covers over a multitude of sins" (1 P 4:8).

It is important not to fall into "ritualism"—the vice of rite-for-rite's-sake. We praise God, we sing his marvelous deeds, and we pray, not "ritual*ist*ically," but expressing our conversion "by a life renewed according to the Gospel. . . ." Our conversion of life will prove the truth of the words we proclaim.

The Ritual gives us some suggestions as to the words to use to praise God at the conclusion of the new Rite of Penance. Here are a few of them.

47. After the absolution, the priest continues:
Give thanks to the Lord, for he is good.
The penitent concludes: *His mercy endures forever.*

We are invited to give thanks, and we are clearly told the reason: the Lord's goodness, a goodness the penitent has just experienced in his or her "own flesh" by being forgiven. Many times this same penitent will have reason to return to these motives when he or she proclaims the everlastingness of God's mercy throughout life.

Then the priest dismisses the penitent who has been reconciled, saying:
The Lord has freed you from your sins. Go in peace.

How often Jesus himself did this! "Go and sin no more. . . ."

In place of this little formula of praise to God and this dismissal, there are other suggested prayers for this purpose in the Ritual as well. All combine the same two ideas of praise for God's forgiveness and dismissal in peace. All leave in the heart of the pardoned Christian the sweet taste of the mercy he or she hoped for, and now will carry through life. Let us look at these alternative formulae.

93. In place of the proclamation of God's praise and the dismissal, the priest may say:
May the Passion of our Lord Jesus Christ,
the intercession of the Blessed Virgin Mary and of all the saints,

whatever good you do and suffering you endure,
heal your sins,
help you grow in holiness,
and reward you with eternal life.
Go in peace.

It is the Passion of Our Lord Jesus Christ that is the principal cause of our forgiveness.

The Church unites itself to the intercession of the one true Mediator, Jesus Christ, through the intercession of its saints.

Every good work done, every cross borne with patience, will endorse both this negative action of washing away our evil, and the positive movement of growth in grace.

It is not just forgiveness-now that we are interested in. We have sought and found a pardon that will be the anticipation of that definitive, final pardon that one day will open to us the grace of a Life that will never have an end.

Or:
The Lord has freed you from sin.
May he bring you safely to his kingdom in heaven.
R/. *Amen.*

Freedom comes to us from God.

Final, definitive salvation will be bestowed in "his kingdom in heaven."

There, we shall glorify him with the canticle of those in love. Here below, having experienced the living marvel of his forgiveness, we also praise him and proclaim his glory.

Or:
Blessed are those
whose sins have been forgiven,
whose evil deeds have been forgotten.
Rejoice in the Lord,
and go in peace.

Happy the one who is restored to a "normal" life—the life of grace! Where injustice and unrighteousness have reigned, now there is justification from a God who forgives our offenses.

We rejoice in this justice of God within us. Now we can go in peace—the peace which God grants his sons and daughters.

Or:

Go in peace,
and proclaim to the world
the wonderful works of God,
who has brought you salvation.

We are going back to the street, into the trenches, to fight for peace.

Every Christian, everyone who has felt God's mercy in his or her misery, is to be a prophet: a messenger of the goodness of God.

The greatest of the mighty deeds of God is Christ Jesus, our Savior.

The celebration of Reconciliation is completed. We have examined our conscience, and made the preparatory prayer. There has been contrition, confession and absolution. We have given thanks to God for the marvels he continues to work in the midst of his people. Now we must make satisfaction for our faults—not only by performing the sacramental penance imposed, but by being docile to the movements of the Spirit, who seeks to mold us in the image of Christ.

We are returning to our home, to our work, to our life of interaction with our neighbor. In every action of our life, we shall be faced with a variety of paths to follow—God's path, and paths which are not his. His is the narrow one, the arduous one. The others are usually attractive, as the Sirens' song was attractive to old Ulysses, in Greek mythology, and it draws our vessel toward the shoals.

God grant the precious gift of a life of repentance to all who use this book. May they know that without Him we can do nothing—and that we can do all things in Him who strengthens us.

Conclusion

We have completed what we set out to do when we began to examine our consciences. We have finished the arduous and painful course that led us to a knowledge of who we are. We have had to face temptations along the way. We were tempted to think that all this examination and review of our lives would do no good. "Everything will still be the same," we said. But no, with watchfulness and prayer, we came to understand that we could be on guard against the devil, that "roaring lion looking for someone to devour" (1 P 5:8-9). Dangers there surely were. But the very dangers put us on the alert and we no longer needed to fall into them. At every moment, we had the certainty that God would not permit us to be tempted beyond our strength (cf. 1 Cor 10:13). As penitents on the way to conversion, we were happy at having received the strength to stand fast in the moment of trial (cf. Jm 1:12). We knew that there were sins that lead to death (cf. 1 Jn 5:16), and that it would profit us nothing if we gained the whole world and suffered the loss of our soul (cf. Mt 16:16).

But we knew our weakness, too. We were aware of the fragile nature of our strength, and that there were slight sins, of the kind "with which one cannot live," as St. Augustine said. We did not deceive ourselves. And yet our consciences, with all their delicacy, had now been formed aright, and did not quail or lose their peace in the face of the thousand imperfections that well up in our lives every day that we live them.

On every page of this book, we have learned that we are sinners—that we have need of repentance, and of bitter tears for our guilty deeds, like those of Peter weeping and gaining redemption from his sins (cf. Lk 22:61-62). We learned that there is a price to pay for this redemption, this rescue: the price of prayer, fasting, alms, joy in suffering, and a life of the works of mercy, in imitation of the merciful Christ.

If, at this moment, the reader knows with a deep, interior assent that there is more joy in heaven for one sinner who repents than for ninety-nine who have no need of repentance (cf. Lk 15:7), then this book will have been worth something. If he or she has come to a realization that our only valid definition in the eyes of the Father who awaits us at the bend in the road is that of his prodigal sons and daughters—hungry, naked, struggling back from a land of exile, but knowing the way home—then this book will have been worth something.

"Delay not your conversion to the Lord, put it not off from day to day" (Si 5:8). Let us not postpone the moment of the Lord's embrace, and His kiss of peace.